The De...

Herbs and Spices

Copyright © 2024 T D Bellucci

All rights reserved.

Contents

Ajwain 2	Chili pepper 70	Hoja santa 136
Alexanders 4	Chironji 72	Horseradish 138
Alkanet 6	Chives 74	Huacatay 140
Alligator pepper 8	Cicely 76	Hyssop 142
Allspice 10	Cilantro (coriander) 78	Jasmine 144
Angelica 12	Cinnamon 80	Jakhya 146
Anise 14	Cinnamon myrtle 82	Jalapeño 148
Aniseed myrtle 16	Clary 84	Jimbu 150
Annatto 18	Clove 86	Juniper berry 152
Artemisia 20	Coriander seed 88	Kaffir lime 154
Asafoetida 22	Coriander, Vietnamese	Kala zeera 156
Avens 24	 90	Keluak 158
Avocado leaf 26	Costmary 92	Kencur 160
Barberry 28	Cubeb pepper 94	Kinh gioi 162
Basil 30	Culantro 96	Kokum 164
Basil, Holy 32	Cumin 98	Korarima 166
Basil, lemon 34	Curry leaf 100	Koseret leaves 168
Basil, Thai 36	Cyperus articulates .. 102	Kudum Puli 170
Bay leaf 38	Dill 104	Kutjera 172
Blue fenugreek 40	Dill seed 106	Lavender 174
Boldo 42	Elderflower 108	Lemon balm 176
Borage 44	Epazote 110	Lemon ironbark 178
California bay laurel .. 46	Fennel 112	Lemon myrtle 180
Cao guo 48	Fenugreek 114	Lemon verbena 182
Caper 50	Filé powder 116	Lemongrass 184
Caraway 52	Fingerroot 118	Lesser calamint 186
Cardamom 54	Galangal, greater 120	Licorice (liquorice) ... 188
Cardamom, black 56	Galangal, lesser 122	Lovage leaves 190
Cassia 58	Garlic 124	Lovage seeds 192
Cayenne pepper 60	Garlic chives 126	Locust beans 194
Celery leaf 62	Ginger 128	Mace 196
Celery seed 64	Golpar 130	Mahleb 198
Chervil 66	Grains of paradise ... 132	Marjoram 200
Chicory 68	Grains of Selim 134	Mastic 202

Mint 204	Pepper, long 256	Sorrel 306
Mountain horopito ... 206	Pepper, mountain 258	Spearmint 308
Musk mallow 208	Peppermint 260	Spikenard 310
Mustard, black 210	Peppermint gum leaf	Star anise 312
Mustard, brown 212	 262	Stone parsley 314
Mustard, white 214	Perilla 264	Sumac 316
Mustard, yellow 216	Peruvian pepper 266	Sweet woodruff 318
New Mexico chile 218	Pipicha 268	Tarragon 320
Nigella sativa 220	Poppy seed 270	Tasmanian pepper ... 322
Njangsa 222	Purslane 272	Thyme 324
Nutmeg 224	Quassia 274	Tonka beans 326
Olida 226	Red rice powder 276	Turmeric 328
Oregano 228	Rice paddy herb 278	Vanilla 330
Oregano, Cuban 230	Rosemary 280	Voatsiperifery 332
Oregano, Greek 232	Rue 282	Wasabi 334
Orris root 234	Safflower 284	Water-pepper 336
Pandan flower 236	Saffron 286	Wattleseed 338
Pandan leaf 238	Sage 288	Wild thyme 340
Pápalo 240	Salad burnet 290	Wintergreen 342
Paprika 242	Sassafras 292	Wood avens 344
Paracress 244	Sesame Seed 294	Woodruff 346
Parsley 246	Savory, summer 296	Wormwood 348
Pennyroyal 248	Savory, winter 298	Yerba Buena 350
Pepper 250	Shiso 300	Yarrow 352
Pepper, Brazilian 252	Sichuan pepper 302	Za'atar 354
Pepper, Dorrigo 254	Silphium 304	Zedoary 356

Welcome to a world where flavor meets tradition, and nature's bounty is at your fingertips. The Definitive Guide to Herbs and Spices is your essential companion through the garden of over 170 herbs and spices that have seasoned our meals and healed our bodies for centuries. With each page, uncover vibrant illustrations that bring the essence of each herb and spice to life, followed by insights into their culinary uses, health benefits, cultural roots, and the journey from field to kitchen. Whether you're a professional chef or a home cook, this guide promises to enrich your understanding and inspire your palate. Let's embark on this flavorful journey together, exploring the spices and herbs that make our cuisine diverse and our lives healthier.

Ajwain

Ajwain, also known as carom seeds or bishop's weed, is an herb in the family Apiaceae. Botanically known as Trachyspermum ammi, ajwain is indigenous to the eastern regions of the Mediterranean, possibly Egypt, and now also cultivated in India, Iran, and Afghanistan. The seeds are small, oval, and ridged, resembling cumin or caraway seeds in appearance.

Culinary Uses

Ajwain has a pungent and slightly bitter flavor with a distinctive aroma similar to thyme, as it contains thymol. It is commonly used in Indian and Middle Eastern cooking, particularly for flavoring bread, biscuits, and pastries as well as in bean dishes. It pairs well with other spices like turmeric, paprika, fennel, and coriander.

Medicinal properties

Ajwain is reputed for its antiseptic, fungicide, anesthetic, and anti-inflammatory properties. It is traditionally used to relieve indigestion, colic, and various respiratory ailments. The seeds are thought to have health benefits including aiding in weight loss, improving cholesterol levels, and reducing blood pressure.

Cultural Significance

Ajwain holds a significant place in Indian Ayurvedic medicine and is often used in rituals and ceremonies as a symbol of protection due to its potent properties. In some cultures, ajwain seeds are thought to bring good luck and are used in various traditional practices.

Production

The plant thrives in arid and semi-arid conditions, which is why it is predominantly cultivated in the Indian subcontinent and Iran. India is the largest producer and consumer of ajwain. The economics of ajwain trade are significant in the spice markets where it's valued for its medicinal and culinary uses.

Other facts

Ajwain seeds are often chewed on their own or with a mixture of other seeds and spices, like fennel, for digestive benefits. The oil extracted from ajwain seeds is used in various cosmetic and pharmaceutical products. Additionally, ajwain is sometimes used as a deterrent for pests due to its strong aroma.

Alexanders

Alexanders is an aromatic plant that was once a prevalent herb but is now largely forgotten in the culinary world. Botanically known as Smyrnium olusatrum, Alexanders is part of the Apiaceae family. Originating from the Mediterranean region, it has spread throughout Europe and parts of Asia. The plant is robust, with a stout stem, large leaves, and small yellow-green flowers that give way to black seeds.

Culinary Uses

Alexanders has a flavor similar to celery or parsley with a slightly bitter aftertaste. Historically, it was used in a variety of dishes, including soups, stews, and salads. The stems, leaves, and roots were all edible. It was often paired with other robust herbs and spices such as garlic, dill, and fennel. In ancient Rome, it was a common kitchen garden plant before being replaced by celery.

Medicinal properties

In traditional medicine, Alexanders was used for various ailments due to its diuretic and digestive properties. It was believed to help with liver and spleen diseases and was a common treatment for general indigestion and flatulence.

Cultural Significance

In ancient cultures, Alexanders was sometimes used in feasting and was considered a protective plant. Its use in cultural rituals has declined along with its culinary use, but it was once a symbol of prosperity and was likely used in early culinary and medicinal practices.

Production

Currently, Alexanders is not cultivated on a commercial scale and is not significant in international trade. It can be found growing wild in coastal regions and is occasionally cultivated in heritage and private gardens for personal use or by historical cooking enthusiasts.

Alkanet

Alkanet, not commonly recognized as a culinary spice, is primarily known for its natural dye properties and has some historical medicinal uses. Alkanet, with the botanical name Alkanna tinctoria, belongs to the borage family (Boraginaceae). It is native to the Mediterranean region. The plant is characterized by its red roots and small blue flowers. The roots contain a red dye called alkannin, which is used for coloring.

Culinary Uses

The culinary uses of alkanet are limited due to its potent coloring properties and bitter taste. Historically, it has been used more as a food dye than as a spice. It imparts a ruby red color to fats, which is why it's sometimes used to tint oils and wines. When used in foods, it's typically in combination with other spices or ingredients that can mask its bitterness, such as in spiced cakes or sweet dishes.

Medicinal properties

Traditionally, alkanet has been used for its potential benefits in treating wounds and skin problems due to its anti-inflammatory and antimicrobial properties. It has been applied externally as a poultice or infused in oils for treating burns and other skin irritations.

Cultural Significance

In the past, alkanet root was valued for its dye and was often used to color fabrics and cosmetics. It has been used in various cultural ceremonies and rituals for its vibrant color, which could symbolize passion or life due to its deep red hue.

Production

Alkanet is not cultivated on a large scale for trade, as its use is rather specialized. It is typically harvested from the wild or grown in small quantities in herb gardens. The production and trade of alkanet are mostly for its use in natural dyes rather than as a spice.

Alligator pepper

Alligator pepper, known for its unique, spicy flavor, is a West African spice made from the seeds of the Aframomum melegueta plant. Aframomum melegueta is a species in the ginger family, Zingiberaceae. The plant is native to swamps and damp habitats along the West African coast. It grows to about 1-2 meters in height, with long, slender leaves and trumpet-shaped, purple flowers that develop into pods containing the pungent seeds.

Culinary Uses

Alligator pepper has a hot, pungent taste with a hint of cardamom and citrus. It's used in West African cuisine to season foods like soups, stews, meats, and poultry. In terms of combinations, it pairs well with other regional spices such as nutmeg, cloves, and cinnamon. It's also a component of the West African spice blend 'suya', which is used to season grilled meats.

Medicinal properties

In traditional African medicine, alligator pepper is used for its supposed antimicrobial and anti-inflammatory properties. It's believed to aid digestion, serve as a stimulant, and help with conditions such as sore throat and nausea. The seeds are also used for their diuretic effect.

Cultural Significance

Alligator pepper is deeply ingrained in West African culture and is used in rituals and ceremonies, such as naming ceremonies, weddings, and traditional festivals. It symbolizes hospitality and is often presented to guests in social gatherings.

Production

The spice is mostly cultivated in countries along the Gulf of Guinea, including Ghana, Nigeria, and Ivory Coast. It is often found in local markets and is increasingly available in international markets, primarily through specialty spice vendors. Its trade contributes to the local economies of the regions where it is produced.

Other facts

The name 'alligator pepper' comes from the appearance of the seed pods, which are wrinkled and resemble the back of an alligator. While it is primarily known in West Africa, its use has spread to other parts of the world, especially in diasporic communities, as a flavoring agent and cultural symbol. It's also sometimes used as a substitute for grains of paradise, a related spice.

Allspice

Allspice is a celebrated spice known for its distinctive flavor that resembles a combination of cinnamon, nutmeg, and cloves. Allspice comes from the dried berries of the Pimenta dioica tree, a member of the myrtle family. This tree is native to the Greater Antilles, southern Mexico, and Central America. The name "allspice" was coined by the English, who thought it combined the flavor of cinnamon, nutmeg, and cloves.

Culinary Uses

Allspice has a warm, sweet, and spicy flavor. It is a versatile spice used in a variety of dishes ranging from sweet to savory. Common in Caribbean, Middle Eastern, and Latin American cuisines, it's a staple in Jamaican jerk seasoning, Middle Eastern kibbeh, and in many dessert recipes like pies and puddings. It pairs well with other spices such as ginger, thyme, and garlic.

Medicinal properties

Historically, allspice has been used to aid digestion and relieve gas. Its eugenol content may have analgesic and antiseptic properties, making it beneficial for dental hygiene and as a remedy for minor pains and aches.

Cultural Significance

Allspice is integral to many cultural dishes and is often used in holiday foods, such as Christmas pudding and mulled wine, symbolizing warmth and festivity. In Caribbean cultures, it's a cornerstone spice that's integral to the identity of their cuisine.

Production

Jamaica is historically known as the largest producer of allspice and it remains an important export product for the country, though it is also cultivated in other Central American countries and areas with similar climates. The berries are picked when green and unripe and traditionally dried in the sun.

Other facts

Allspice is also called "Jamaica pepper" and was one of the most important spices traded during the spice trade era. Apart from culinary uses, it's also used in the cosmetic industry for fragrances and in the production of some pharmaceuticals. The leaves of the Pimenta dioica are also used in cooking for their aromatic qualities.

Angelica

Angelica is an aromatic herb known for its sweetly scented edible stems and roots that are used in various culinary and medicinal applications. Angelica archangelica, commonly known as garden angelica, is the most widely-used species of the genus Angelica in the Apiaceae family. It is native to northern Europe and certain parts of Asia. The plant can grow up to 2 meters in height and is distinguishable by its large bipinnate leaves and spherical clusters of greenish-white flowers.

Culinary Uses

Angelica has a flavor profile that is sweet and earthy, with hints of celery and licorice. It is used in the culinary world for its stalks and leaves as well as its seeds. The stems can be candied and used as decoration for desserts or baked goods. The leaves are often used to flavor liqueurs like Chartreuse and Benedictine, and the seeds are used in the preparation of some vermouths and gins. It pairs well with fish and is sometimes used in jams and preserves.

Medicinal properties

In traditional medicine, angelica is valued for its potential to aid digestion, relieve flatulence, and expectorate phlegm. It has been used to help with various ailments, including colds, congestion, and rheumatism. Angelica contains compounds such as terpenes and coumarins, which are believed to contribute to its medicinal effects.

Cultural Significance

Angelica has a rich history in folklore and traditional medicine. It was once believed to ward off evil spirits and was associated with the Archangel Michael, which is how it got its name. The plant has been used in rituals and is often planted in traditional medicinal and herb gardens.

Production

Though not widely cultivated on a commercial scale, angelica is grown in northern European countries and has a niche market, particularly for its use in liqueurs and confectionery. The roots and seeds are also traded in small quantities for their use in traditional herbal remedies.

Other facts

Aside from its culinary and medicinal uses, angelica is also appreciated for its ornamental value in gardens. The essential oil derived from angelica is used in perfumery and aromatherapy. In the past, it was also used to make a natural green dye for textiles.

Anise

Anise, also known as aniseed, is a flowering plant whose seeds are used for their distinct flavor and medicinal properties. Anise (Pimpinella anisum) belongs to the Apiaceae family. This herb is native to the Eastern Mediterranean region and Southwest Asia. Anise plants grow to about a meter tall and produce flowers and a small white fruit, commonly referred to as a seed.

Culinary Uses

Aniseed has a sweet, aromatic taste that is reminiscent of licorice. It is used widely in baking and in the production of confectionery, as well as in liquors like ouzo, anisette, and sambuca. In cooking, aniseed flavors dishes like Indian curries, Middle Eastern stews, and Mexican atole. It complements spices like cinnamon, cardamom, and cloves.

Medicinal properties

Anise has been used medicinally to treat digestive issues, relieve cramps, and reduce nausea. Its expectorant properties make it helpful in treating coughs and colds. The essential oil of anise, anethole, is known to have antifungal and antibacterial properties.

Cultural Significance

Aniseed holds significance in various cultures for its perceived ability to ward off the evil eye and is used in rituals and ceremonies. It has been used historically in traditional medicines and was once used to pay taxes. The seed is also associated with certain Greek and Roman customs, such as wedding cakes and feast-day bread.

Production

Anise is cultivated in many parts of the world, with the main producers being India, Turkey, and Spain. It is traded globally, primarily as a spice and flavoring agent. The market for aniseed is relatively stable, with demand driven by both culinary and medicinal uses.

Other facts

Aniseed is often confused with star anise, which is similar in flavor but comes from a different plant. Anise can be used in its whole seed form or ground to a powder. The seeds are also used to flavor teas and are a component in some herbal blends.

Aniseed myrtle

Anise myrtle, also known as aniseed myrtle or ringwood, is an Australian native spice known for its aniseed or licorice flavor. Anise myrtle (Syzygium anisatum) is a rainforest tree that belongs to the Myrtaceae family. Indigenous to the subtropical rainforests of central and south-eastern Queensland, Australia, the tree can grow up to 45 meters tall. The leaves are used to produce an essential oil and as a dried spice.

Culinary Uses

Anise myrtle has a strong licorice flavor with a hint of aniseed, which is why it is used in desserts, sweet dishes, syrups, and glazes. It complements fruits or can be used in baking bread and making tea. In terms of spice combinations, it pairs well with other warm spices such as cinnamon and star anise. It is also used in savory dishes, like sauces and marinades for meat, where its sweet-spicy flavor can shine.

Medicinal properties

Traditionally, Indigenous Australians have used anise myrtle for its antifungal and antibacterial properties. It is also said to have antioxidant benefits and to be a source of lutein, magnesium, and calcium. Modern herbalists sometimes use it to treat indigestion and other digestive issues.

Cultural Significance

Anise myrtle has been part of the diet of Indigenous Australians for thousands of years. While it doesn't have a wide array of known rituals and ceremonial uses, its significance lies in its place as a traditional bush food with cultural and nutritional importance.

Production

Anise myrtle is not widely cultivated on a global scale, and its production is mostly limited to Australia. It is considered a specialty spice and is usually found in boutique spice shops or used by chefs interested in native Australian cuisine.

Other facts

Anise myrtle is often used as a more sustainable substitute for true aniseed or star anise. The essential oil derived from anise myrtle leaves is used in aromatherapy and the cosmetic industry for its fragrance. The tree itself is also valued for its ornamental properties, with attractive foliage and a pleasant aroma.

Annatto

Annatto is a vibrant spice derived from the seeds of the achiote tree, primarily used for its coloring properties. Botanically named Bixa orellana, annatto is a tropical tree from the family Bixaceae. Native to tropical regions from Mexico to Brazil, it's often found in subtropical and tropical areas worldwide. Annatto seeds are encased in bright red pods and are known for the natural pigment they produce called bixin.

Culinary Uses

Annatto's flavor is slightly sweet and peppery with a hint of nuttiness. It's mainly used as a natural coloring agent to impart a yellow to red hue to foods like cheeses (e.g., Cheddar, Red Leicester), margarine, butter, rice, smoked fish, and baked goods. It can also be found in Latin American, Caribbean, and Filipino cuisines, in spice mixes, and for marinating meats. Annatto is sometimes combined with spices such as cumin, chili, and coriander.

Medicinal properties

In traditional medicine, annatto is used for its potential antioxidant properties and as a digestive aid. It has been employed to treat heartburn, stomach discomfort, and high cholesterol. The seeds have been used topically to address skin issues due to their antifungal and antimicrobial properties.

Cultural Significance

Annatto holds cultural importance in Latin America and the Caribbean, where it's often used in traditional dishes and rituals. Historically, it was used as body paint, sunscreen, and insect repellent by indigenous peoples, and as a dye for textiles. In various cultures, annatto is a symbol of health and good fortune.

Production

Annatto is primarily produced in tropical climates where the achiote tree grows. Major producing countries include Peru, Brazil, Kenya, and the Dominican Republic. The seeds are exported globally, mainly for use in food coloring and the cosmetic industry.

Other facts

Aside from its culinary use, annatto is used in the cosmetic industry for lipstick and blush due to its vibrant pigment. In the food industry, it is labeled as E160b as a food additive. The dye from annatto can be extracted by grinding the seeds or steeping them in oil or water.

Artemisia

Artemisia refers to a genus of plants known for their aromatic leaves and medicinal properties. Among them, some species are used as spices in various culinary traditions. The Artemisia genus includes a wide range of plants, such as wormwood (Artemisia absinthium), mugwort (Artemisia vulgaris), and tarragon (Artemisia dracunculus). These plants are part of the Asteraceae family and are native to temperate regions of the Northern Hemisphere, with some species found in Asia and Africa. Artemisias are characterized by their silvery-green foliage, aromatic scent, and bitter taste.

Culinary Uses

Tarragon, one of the most culinary-used Artemisia species, has a distinctive anise-like flavor and is a key ingredient in French cuisine, especially in béarnaise sauce. It's used in a variety of dishes including chicken, fish, and egg dishes, and is often paired with lemon, vinegar, or mustard. Mugwort and wormwood have more bitter flavors and are traditionally used in Asian and European cuisines respectively, often in teas, soups, and as flavorings for meats. Wormwood is famously used in the production of absinthe.

Medicinal properties

Artemisia species have been used in traditional medicine across many cultures for centuries. They are known for their digestive, antiparasitic, and antiseptic properties. Wormwood has been used to treat digestive disorders and as a component in the treatment of malaria with the extraction of artemisinin.

Cultural Significance

In many cultures, Artemisia plants have symbolic meanings, often associated with protection and health. Mugwort, for example, has been used in protective rituals and is believed to ward off evil spirits in some European folklore. Wormwood's association with absinthe gives it a cultural mystique, linked to the bohemian lifestyle of late 19th and early 20th century Europe.

Production

Tarragon is widely cultivated for culinary use, especially in France and the United States. Wormwood and mugwort are often harvested from the wild, though some cultivation occurs for medicinal and culinary purposes.

Asafoetida

Asafoetida, often referred to as "hing," is a potent spice known for its strong sulfuric smell, which transforms into a delightful, onion-like flavor when cooked. Derived from the resinous gum of the Ferula plants, specifically Ferula assa-foetida, this spice is native to Iran and Afghanistan, with significant cultivation also occurring in India. The plant belongs to the Apiaceae family and can grow up to 2 meters tall. Asafoetida is harvested by making incisions in the plant's roots and stems to extract the gum, which is then dried and processed into the spice.

Culinary Uses

Asafoetida's unique flavor is a staple in many Indian, Middle Eastern, and vegetarian cuisines, acting as a replacement for onion and garlic. It's used in a variety of dishes, including lentil curries, soups, stews, and pickles. Asafoetida pairs well with turmeric, cumin, and mustard seeds, enhancing the flavors of vegetables and legumes.

Medicinal properties

In traditional medicine, asafoetida is prized for its digestive properties, often used to relieve gas, bloating, and irritable bowel syndrome (IBS). It also has anti-inflammatory, antiviral, and antibiotic effects. Historically, it was used to combat influenza and respiratory conditions due to its expectorant properties.

Cultural Significance

Asafoetida holds a significant place in Indian Ayurvedic medicine for its health benefits and is also used in rituals and spiritual practices for its supposed protective qualities against evil spirits. In some cultures, it's believed to ward off negative energy and is used in various traditional ceremonies.

Production

The primary producers of asafoetida are Iran and Afghanistan, with India being a major importer and consumer. The spice's production is labor-intensive, as it involves collecting and processing the gum from wild Ferula plants.

Other facts

Due to its pungent odor, asafoetida must be stored in airtight containers to prevent its aroma from affecting other spices or foods. The spice is available in both solid blocks and powdered form, with the latter often being mixed with wheat flour or rice flour to make it easier to use.

Avens

Avens, also known as Geum urbanum or wood avens, is a perennial herb that is part of the rose family (Rosaceae). Though not as widely known or used as other spices, avens has a history of culinary and medicinal use. Avens is native to Europe, North Africa, and Western Asia. It grows in woods and shady places, bearing yellow flowers from May to August. The plant reaches a height of up to 60 cm and is recognized by its hairy stems and pinnate leaves. The root, which is used as a spice, emits a clove-like aroma when dried.

Culinary Uses

The root of avens has a spicy, slightly bitter flavor with a hint of cloves. Historically, it was used to flavor beverages, soups, and medieval European dishes. Although its use in modern cuisine is rare, it can still be found in herbal tea blends and as a natural flavoring agent in some traditional recipes. It pairs well with sweet and savory dishes alike, offering a unique flavor profile reminiscent of cloves and cinnamon.

Medicinal properties

Traditionally, avens has been valued for its antiseptic, astringent, and digestive properties. It has been used to treat gastrointestinal issues, sore throats, and even to help with fever and infectious diseases. The root contains tannins and eugenol, contributing to its medicinal effects.

Cultural Significance

In medieval times, avens was believed to offer protection against evil spirits and was used in various rituals for this purpose. It was also planted around homes and churches as a symbol of protection.

Production

Today, avens is not commercially cultivated on a large scale and is more commonly harvested from the wild for personal use or small-scale herbal production. Its trade is limited, primarily found within herbal and specialty markets.

Other facts

The flowers of avens are attractive to bees and other pollinators, making it a beneficial plant for biodiversity in gardens and wild spaces. In addition to its root, the leaves of avens are sometimes used in salads and have a mild flavor. The plant's name, "Geum," is derived from the Greek word "geno," meaning "to yield an agreeable fragrance," referring to the aromatic quality of its roots.

Avocado leaf

Avocado leaf, derived from the avocado tree (Persea americana), is a lesser-known spice with a unique flavor profile, used in various culinary traditions, particularly in Mexican cuisine. The avocado tree belongs to the Lauraceae family, native to south-central Mexico. It is a large tree that can grow up to 20 meters tall, widely known for its fruit, the avocado. However, the leaves of the avocado tree are also used as a spice, especially in traditional Mexican dishes. These leaves are harvested from the tree, dried, and then used whole or ground.

Culinary Uses

Avocado leaves impart a subtle anise-like flavor with hints of licorice and slight nuttiness, making them an excellent addition to soups, stews, beans, and grilled meats. They are particularly famous for flavoring black beans in Mexican cuisine. The leaves can be used whole, similar to bay leaves, or ground into a powder and added to dishes. They combine well with other traditional Mexican spices and herbs, such as cumin, chili peppers, and cilantro, enhancing the complexity of flavors in the dish.

Medicinal properties

Traditionally, avocado leaves have been used in folk medicine for their supposed health benefits. They are believed to have anticonvulsant, antimicrobial, and antioxidant properties. Infusions made from avocado leaves are used to treat stomachaches, diarrhea, and kidney stones.

Cultural Significance

In Mexican culture, avocado leaves are an essential part of culinary heritage, especially in the preparation of traditional dishes. They are used not only for their flavor but also for their medicinal properties, reflecting the deep-rooted tradition of using natural remedies for health and wellness.

Production

Avocado leaves are primarily harvested from avocado trees grown for their fruit. Mexico, being the largest producer of avocados in the world, is also a significant source of avocado leaves used for culinary purposes.

Other facts

When using avocado leaves in cooking, it's important to source them from edible varieties of avocado trees, as leaves from some varieties can be toxic. In addition to their use in traditional dishes, avocado leaves can also be brewed into a tea, offering a soothing and aromatic beverage.

Barberry

Barberry is a spice derived from the fruit of the Berberis vulgaris plant, known for its vibrant color and tart flavor. Barberry belongs to the Berberidaceae family and is native to Europe, Asia, the Middle East, and North Africa. The plant is a deciduous shrub that can grow up to 4 meters tall, with yellow flowers and elongated red berries. The berries are harvested and dried for culinary and medicinal use.

Culinary Uses

Barberries, or "zereshk" in Persian cuisine, have a sharp, tart flavor that adds a burst of color and taste to dishes. They are a staple in Iranian cooking, most notably used in zereshk polo, a dish of rice, barberries, and chicken. Barberries can be used fresh or dried and are often soaked in water to soften before use. They pair well with saffron, cumin, and other Middle Eastern spices and are also added to salads, pilafs, and jams for a hint of sourness.

Medicinal properties

Barberries are rich in vitamins, minerals, and antioxidants, particularly berberine, which has been shown to have antimicrobial, anti-inflammatory, and immune-boosting properties.. Recent studies suggest they may help regulate blood sugar levels and improve cholesterol.

Cultural Significance

In Persian culture, barberries are not just a culinary ingredient but also a symbol of patience and endurance, reflecting the plant's ability to thrive in harsh conditions. They are often used in wedding ceremonies and other celebrations as a symbol of joy and happiness.

Production

Iran is the largest producer and consumer of barberries in the world, with the South Khorasan province being the center of production. The cultivation and harvest of barberries are labor-intensive processes, contributing significantly to the local economy.

Other facts

Aside from their culinary and medicinal uses, barberry plants are also valued for their ornamental qualities, with many varieties cultivated for their attractive foliage and fruit. The shrub's thorns make it an effective barrier plant or hedge in landscaping. Additionally, the berberine in barberries has been used historically to dye wool, leather, and wood.

Basil

Basil, known for its aromatic leaves, is a staple herb in many cuisines worldwide, most notably in Italian and Southeast Asian dishes. Basil (Ocimum basilicum) belongs to the mint family, Lamiaceae, and is native to tropical regions from Central Africa to Southeast Asia. It is an annual herb, characterized by its lush, green leaves, and sometimes purple or red, depending on the variety. There are several types of basil, including sweet basil, Thai basil, and lemon basil, each with its unique flavor profile.

Culinary Uses

Basil's flavor is sweet and peppery, with clove-like notes in some varieties. It is a key ingredient in Italian cuisine, used in pesto, caprese salad, and as a garnish for pizzas and pastas. Thai basil, with its anise-like flavor, is essential in Southeast Asian dishes such as curries, stir-fries, and soups. Basil pairs well with tomatoes, garlic, onion, and other herbs like oregano and rosemary. It is best added at the end of cooking to preserve its flavor and vibrant color.

Medicinal properties

Traditionally, basil has been used for its digestive and anti-inflammatory properties. It contains essential oils such as eugenol, which can help to reduce inflammation and has antibacterial properties. Basil is also rich in antioxidants, which can protect against free radical damage, and vitamin K, which is important for blood clotting.

Cultural Significance

Basil holds a significant place in many cultures. In Italy, it's a symbol of love, while in India, it is sacred to the gods Vishnu and Krishna and is used in religious ceremonies. In various traditions, basil is associated with protection and is planted in gardens or hung in homes to ward off evil spirits.

Production

Italy, the United States (particularly California), and Egypt are among the leading producers of basil. It is cultivated worldwide in temperate climates, both in greenhouses and outdoors. Basil is harvested for its leaves, which are used fresh or dried, and for its essential oil.

Other facts

Basil seeds, known for their health benefits, swell and become gelatinous when soaked in water, similar to chia seeds. Basil is also popular in aromatic oils and perfumes for its fragrant essential oils. To maintain its freshness, basil should be stored in the refrigerator or frozen in ice cube trays with water.

Basil, Holy

Holy Basil, also known as Tulsi, is revered as a sacred herb in India and has significant religious, medicinal, and culinary importance. Holy Basil (Ocimum sanctum or Ocimum tenuiflorum) belongs to the Lamiaceae family. It is an aromatic perennial plant native to the Indian subcontinent but now grown in many tropical regions of Asia. Unlike common basil (Ocimum basilicum), Holy Basil has a more clove-like aroma due to its high eugenol content. The plant can grow up to 60 cm tall, with hairy stems, green or purple leaves, and purple flowers.

Culinary Uses

Holy Basil's flavor is spicy and peppery, with notes of clove and mint. While not as commonly used in culinary applications as other types of basil, it is occasionally added to Thai dishes, soups, and stir-fries for its distinctive flavor. It pairs well with spicy foods and can be used in herbal teas, both for its taste and therapeutic properties.

Medicinal properties

Holy Basil is highly valued in Ayurvedic medicine for its adaptogenic properties, helping the body adapt to stress and promoting mental balance. It is believed to have anti-inflammatory, antibacterial, antiviral, and antioxidant properties. Commonly used to treat colds, headaches, stomach disorders, inflammation, heart disease, poisoning, and malaria.

Cultural Significance

In Hinduism, Holy Basil is considered a manifestation of the goddess Lakshmi and is worshipped as a sacred plant. It is commonly grown in household gardens and temples, and its leaves are used in daily rituals. The plant symbolizes purity, happiness, love, and devotion.

Production

Holy Basil is predominantly grown in India, Nepal, and parts of Southeast Asia. While not a major commercial crop outside these regions, its cultivation is spreading with the global interest in herbal and natural remedies.

Other facts

Holy Basil is also known for its environmental significance, as it is used in organic farming practices for pest management. The seeds of the plant can be used to make a cooling and nutritious drink, similar to basil seeds from other varieties. In traditional medicine, every part of the plant—leaves, stem, and seeds—is used for therapeutic purposes.

Basil, lemon

Lemon basil, a unique and fragrant variety of basil, is cherished for its distinctive lemon aroma and flavor, adding a citrusy twist to culinary creations. Lemon basil (Ocimum × citriodorum) is a hybrid between basil (Ocimum basilicum) and African basil (Ocimum americanum). It is characterized by its bright green leaves and a strong lemon scent, attributed to its high concentration of citral, a natural compound also found in lemon oil. This variety is particularly popular in Southeast Asian and Middle Eastern cuisines.

Culinary Uses

Lemon basil's flavor profile combines the herbaceousness of basil with the zest of lemon, making it an excellent addition to salads, fish dishes, poultry, and teas. It is especially favored in Indonesian, Thai, and Laotian cuisines, where it's used in soups, stir-fries, and curries. Lemon basil pairs well with other herbs and spices such as cilantro, mint, chili, and garlic. It can also be used to infuse oils and vinegars or to make a refreshing lemon basil sorbet.

Medicinal properties

While not as widely studied for its medicinal properties as other basil varieties, lemon basil is believed to share similar benefits, including digestive and anti-inflammatory effects. Its essential oils are thought to have antimicrobial properties, and the herb is traditionally used in some cultures to relieve stomachaches and gas.

Cultural Significance

Lemon basil holds a special place in the culinary traditions of the regions where it is extensively used. In Indonesia, it is an essential ingredient in 'nasi ulam', a ceremonial dish. Its unique flavor and aroma also symbolize freshness and purity in culinary practices.

Production

Lemon basil is primarily grown in tropical and subtropical climates, with Indonesia, Thailand, and parts of the Middle East being notable producers. It is cultivated both commercially and in home gardens. The herb prefers warm weather and well-drained soil to thrive.

Other facts

Lemon basil's leaves are smaller and more narrow compared to those of sweet basil. It flowers more quickly, which means it requires regular harvesting to prevent it from going to seed too early. To preserve its lemony scent and flavor, lemon basil is best used fresh rather than dried.

Basil, Thai

Thai basil, a key ingredient in Southeast Asian cuisine, is renowned for its unique flavor that combines hints of anise with a slight spiciness, setting it apart from other basil varieties. Thai basil (Ocimum basilicum var. thyrsiflora) is a variety of basil native to Southeast Asia. It has small, narrow leaves, purple stems, and a distinctive aroma reminiscent of anise or licorice. Unlike sweet basil, Thai basil is more resilient to cooking and retains its flavor when subjected to high temperatures, making it ideal for hot dishes.

Culinary Uses

Thai basil's robust flavor profile makes it a staple in many Thai dishes, including curries, stir-fries, and salads. It is a crucial ingredient in the famous Thai dish pad krapow (stir-fried meat with Thai basil). Thai basil pairs well with ingredients like chili peppers, garlic, ginger, and coconut milk, enhancing the complexity of flavors in a dish. It's also used in Vietnamese cuisine, notably in pho and as a garnish for various soups and noodle dishes.

Medicinal properties

In traditional medicine, Thai basil is valued for its therapeutic properties, including digestive and anti-inflammatory effects. It is believed to have adaptogenic properties, helping the body to combat stress. The herb is also noted for its high antioxidant content, contributing to overall health and well-being.

Cultural Significance

Thai basil holds a significant place in Thai culture, not only as a culinary herb but also for its supposed protective properties. It is often used in religious ceremonies and rituals. The herb symbolizes hospitality and is commonly grown in household gardens, reflecting its importance in Thai daily life.

Production

Thai basil is predominantly grown in Southeast Asia, with Thailand, Vietnam, and Cambodia being major producers. It thrives in warm, tropical climates and is cultivated both for local consumption and international export.

Other facts

Thai basil flowers more readily than sweet basil, producing small, purple blooms that are also edible and often used as a garnish. The plant requires full sun and regular watering to flourish. Harvesting the leaves regularly can help to encourage more bushy growth and prevent the plant from bolting (flowering prematurely), which can affect the flavor of the leaves.

Bay leaf

Bay leaf, a classic culinary herb, is valued for its aromatic influence in a variety of dishes worldwide, imparting a subtle yet distinct flavor profile. Bay leaves come from the laurel tree, Laurus nobilis, a plant native to the Mediterranean region. The leaves are dark green, glossy, and oval-shaped, with a leathery texture. Used both fresh and dried, bay leaves are a staple in cooking due to their aromatic properties, which are released slowly during the cooking process.

Culinary Uses

Bay leaf's flavor is herbal, slightly floral, and somewhat similar to oregano and thyme. It is used in soups, stews, meat dishes, sauces, and stocks, where it imparts a depth of flavor that complements other herbs and spices. Bay leaves are often included in bouquet garni (a bundle of herbs) and are a key ingredient in many Mediterranean, French, and Indian dishes. They are typically removed before serving as they can be a choking hazard and are difficult to digest.

Medicinal properties

Traditionally, bay leaves have been used for their digestive and anti-inflammatory properties. They contain compounds like cineole and eugenol, which have been associated with reducing stress, alleviating arthritis, and supporting the digestive system.

Cultural Significance

In ancient Greece and Rome, bay leaves were symbols of wisdom, peace, and protection. The laurel wreath, made from bay leaves, was a sign of honor and victory, awarded to athletes and poets.

Production

The primary producers of bay leaves are countries in the Mediterranean region, including Turkey, Greece, and Italy, where the climate is ideal for growing laurel trees. The leaves are harvested, dried, and then packaged for culinary use.

Other facts

Bay leaves have a long shelf life when dried and stored properly in a cool, dry place, maintaining their flavor for months or even years. There's a common misconception that bay leaves don't add flavor to dishes, but this is due to their subtle taste profile, which enhances the overall flavor of a dish rather than overpowering it.

Blue fenugreek

Blue fenugreek, also known as blue melilot or sweet trefoil, is a lesser-known spice compared to its cousin, the traditional fenugreek, but it holds a unique place in culinary and medicinal traditions, especially in certain European regions. Blue fenugreek (Trigonella caerulea) is part of the Fabaceae family, closely related to the more common fenugreek (Trigonella foenum-graecum). It is native to the mountainous regions of Eastern Europe and parts of Asia, including Georgia, Armenia, and Azerbaijan. The plant produces small, blue flowers, and its leaves are used both as a herb and spice.

Culinary Uses

Blue fenugreek has a milder, sweeter flavor compared to regular fenugreek, with a hint of nuttiness and a touch of bitterness. It is a key ingredient in traditional Georgian spice mixes, such as khmeli suneli, and is used to flavor cheeses, breads, and sauces in Swiss and Georgian cuisines. Its subtle sweetness enhances vegetable dishes, soups, and stews, and it pairs well with other spices like coriander, cloves, and cinnamon.

Medicinal properties

Traditionally, blue fenugreek has been used for its digestive and anti-inflammatory properties. It is believed to help soothe the stomach, reduce cholesterol levels, and aid in blood sugar regulation. Its seeds and leaves have been used in herbal teas and poultices to treat skin irritations and wounds.

Cultural Significance

In Georgia and Switzerland, blue fenugreek is more than just a culinary herb; it is a symbol of the rich agricultural and culinary heritage of these regions. In Georgia, it is an essential component of the national spice blend khmeli suneli, which is used in many traditional dishes.

Production

The herb is harvested for its leaves and seeds, which are then dried for culinary and medicinal use. Its niche market means it is less commonly found in mainstream spice markets but can be sourced from specialty stores or online suppliers focusing on Eastern European or Swiss products.

Boldo

Boldo is a remarkable herb known for its distinctive aroma and a wide array of medicinal benefits, making it a valued addition to both the culinary and health sectors. Boldo (Peumus boldus) is an evergreen shrub native to the central regions of Chile, belonging to the Monimiaceae family. The plant features oval, leathery leaves that are highly aromatic and small, yellowish-green flowers. It is the leaves of the boldo plant that are used both as a culinary herb and for medicinal purposes.

Culinary Uses

The flavor profile of boldo leaves is strong, with a slightly bitter, peppery taste and a hint of mint. Due to its potent flavor, it is used sparingly in cooking. Boldo leaves are traditionally used to season meats, fish, and in the preparation of teas in South American cuisine. They can also be found in some alcoholic beverages, providing a unique flavor. In culinary applications, boldo is not widely used outside its native region and is often an acquired taste.

Medicinal properties

Boldo leaves are renowned for their health benefits, particularly for the digestive system. They contain boldine, an alkaloid that has been shown to stimulate bile production, aiding in digestion and liver function.

Cultural Significance

In Chile and other parts of South America, boldo has been used for centuries both in traditional medicine and cooking. It holds a significant place in herbal medicine, with its use passed down through generations.

Production

Boldo is primarily harvested from wild plants in the central and southern regions of Chile. While there is some cultivation for commercial purposes, much of the boldo used medicinally and culinary is collected from natural stands. The leaves are harvested, then dried for use in teas and extracts.

Borage

Borage, known for its striking blue flowers and cucumber-like flavor, is a versatile herb that adds a unique touch to culinary dishes and has a range of medicinal benefits. Borage (Borago officinalis) is an annual herb native to the Mediterranean region but has been naturalized in many other areas. It belongs to the Boraginaceae family and is easily recognized by its vibrant blue, star-shaped flowers and hairy leaves and stems. Borage grows up to 60-100 cm in height and is prized for both its decorative and culinary uses.

Culinary Uses

The flavor profile of borage is similar to that of cucumber, making its leaves and flowers a refreshing addition to salads, drinks, and garnishes. The flowers are edible and often used to decorate desserts and cocktails, while the young leaves can be cooked like spinach or added raw to salads. Borage is also used in traditional recipes like the filling for ravioli and as a flavoring in pickles and preserves. It pairs well with fish, poultry, and fresh vegetables.

Medicinal properties

Traditionally it is believed to help with respiratory conditions, reduce fever, and improve skin health. Borage oil is extracted from the seeds and used in supplements to treat conditions such as arthritis, atopic dermatitis, and to maintain healthy skin.

Cultural Significance

In folklore, borage was associated with courage and bravery, and it was believed to bring comfort and joy. It was historically used in wines and drinks intended to uplift spirits and was planted in gardens to attract bees and enhance biodiversity.

Production

Borage is cultivated in gardens and farms primarily for its seeds (for oil production) and flowers (for culinary and decorative uses). It grows well in most temperate climates and is often found in herb gardens for its ease of growing and beneficial effects on surrounding plants and soil.

Other facts

Borage is considered a "companion plant" in vegetable gardens, reputed to repel pests and improve the growth and flavor of nearby plants. The plant is a prolific self-seeder, which means it can easily spread and grow in places where it was previously planted. Care should be taken when handling borage raw due to its small hairs, which can be irritating to sensitive skin.

California bay laurel

California bay laurel, also known by its scientific name Umbellularia californica, is a prominent tree native to the coastal forests of California and parts of the Pacific Northwest. This evergreen tree is not only significant for its ecological role but also for its culinary, medicinal, and cultural contributions. The California bay laurel is an evergreen tree that can grow up to 30 meters tall, characterized by its dense foliage of aromatic leaves. Its leaves are used both as a spice and for their essential oils. The tree bears small yellowish-green flowers and purple berries. The botanical family of California bay laurel is Lauraceae, which it shares with other well-known plants like cinnamon and avocado.

Culinary Uses

The leaves of the California bay laurel are highly aromatic and are used in cooking for their distinct, pungent flavor, which is somewhat similar to but stronger than the Mediterranean bay leaves (Laurus nobilis). They impart a sharp, slightly minty taste with hints of eucalyptus. Commonly used in soups, stews, braises, and marinades, these leaves are versatile in culinary applications. They blend well with other spices, such as thyme, sage, and oregano, enhancing the flavor profile of various dishes. Due to their strong flavor, they are typically used sparingly.

Medicinal Properties

Traditionally, the leaves contain compounds with anti-inflammatory, antimicrobial, and antifungal properties. Herbal remedies often utilize the leaves for treating colds, stomach aches, and rheumatism. Essential oils from the leaves are also used in aromatherapy to relieve stress and anxiety.

Cultural Significance

The California bay laurel holds significant cultural importance in Native American traditions, where it has been used in rituals and ceremonies for purification and healing.

Production

The tree is indigenous to the coastal regions of California and southwestern Oregon. While not widely cultivated on a commercial scale for spice production, the leaves are often harvested from wild trees.

Other Facts

The wood of the California bay laurel tree is valued for its durability and is used in woodworking and furniture making. Despite its culinary uses, the leaves should be used with caution as they can be toxic in large quantities. The tree plays an important ecological role in its native habitats, providing food and shelter for various wildlife species.

Cao guo

Cao Guo, also known as Chinese black cardamom or Tsao-ko, is a distinctive spice commonly used in Chinese and Vietnamese cuisines. Cao Guo (Amomum tsao-ko) is a member of the ginger family, Zingiberaceae, and thrives in the mountainous regions of Southwest China and parts of Southeast Asia. It is a perennial plant characterized by its large, lance-shaped leaves and small, dark brown to black pods that encase the seeds.

Culinary Uses

Cao Guo has a strong, camphor-like aroma with notes of smoke and a hint of mint. The spice is predominantly used in savory dishes, contributing a complex flavor profile to stews, braises, and soups. It is an essential ingredient in Chinese Sichuan and Yunnan cuisines, particularly in recipes for slow-cooked meats and as part of the traditional Chinese five-spice powder. Cao Guo pairs well with other robust spices like star anise, cinnamon, and cloves. Its unique flavor is less suited for fresh applications and is typically used in moderation to avoid overpowering dishes.

Medicinal Properties

In traditional Chinese medicine, Cao Guo is valued for its digestive and warming properties. It is believed to help in dispelling cold, promoting stomach and spleen health, and reducing dampness within the body.

Cultural Significance

While Cao Guo does not hold as wide a cultural significance as some other spices or herbs, it is an important component of regional cuisines and traditional medicine in China. Its use in certain dishes and medicinal formulas reflects the deep-rooted appreciation for the balance of flavors and health benefits in Chinese culture.

Production

Cao Guo is cultivated mainly in the Yunnan and Guangxi provinces of China, where the climate and elevation are ideal for its growth. The spice is harvested from the dried fruits of the plant, which are collected, dried, and cracked open to reveal the aromatic seeds inside.

Other Facts

Cao Guo is often confused with green cardamom; however, they belong to different species within the same family and have distinctly different flavors and uses. Unlike green cardamom, Cao Guo is rarely used in sweet dishes.

Caper

Capers, known for their distinctive tangy and salty flavor, are a beloved ingredient in many Mediterranean dishes. Capers are the unopened flower buds of Capparis spinosa, a perennial plant that belongs to the caper family, Capparaceae. This plant is native to the Mediterranean region and parts of Asia, thriving in harsh conditions, including rocky soils and drought-prone areas. It is characterized by its round, dark green leaves and beautiful white flowers with long, purple stamens.

Culinary Uses

Capers are renowned for their unique, sharp flavor that is both tangy and salty, often compared to a blend of lemon and olives. They are a staple in Mediterranean cuisine, featured in classic dishes such as chicken piccata, tapenade, and puttanesca sauce.. Their piquant flavor pairs well with lemon, garlic, olives, and tomatoes. Capers are typically pickled or salted before use, which enhances their distinct taste and preserves them for longer shelf life. They should be rinsed before use to remove excess saltiness if salt-packed or to balance their brine-pickled tang.

Medicinal Properties

While not as prominently recognized for their medicinal properties as some herbs, capers have been noted for their antioxidant and anti-inflammatory effects. They are rich in flavonoids such as rutin and quercetin, which can help to reduce oxidative stress and may support heart health. Capers also contain vitamins and minerals, including vitamin K.

Cultural Significance

In the Mediterranean region, capers have been used in culinary traditions for thousands of years, appreciated for their bold flavor that can enhance a wide variety of dishes. They are also mentioned in ancient texts, highlighting their long-standing culinary and medicinal use.

Production

Italy, Spain, and Morocco are among the leading producers of capers. The buds must be hand-picked early in the morning. The capers are dried in the sun and then either pickled in vinegar, brine, or packed in salt.

Caraway

Caraway, known for its aromatic seeds, plays a key role in various cuisines across Europe, North Africa, and Western Asia. Caraway (Carum carvi) is a member of the Apiaceae family, which also includes parsley, carrots, and celery. It is a biennial plant, native to Europe, Asia, and North Africa, characterized by its feathery leaves and small, white or pink flowers. The plant is most valued for its crescent-shaped seeds, which have a distinctive, slightly sweet and peppery flavor with anise and licorice undertones.

Culinary Uses

Caraway seeds are celebrated for their unique taste, contributing depth and complexity to dishes. They are a staple in European bread, like rye and pumpernickel, and are used in sauerkraut, soups, cheeses, and as a spice in savory dishes. Caraway seeds are also used in desserts and liqueurs, imparting a warm, earthy flavor. In Middle Eastern cuisines, they flavor meats and vegetables, demonstrating their versatility. The seeds pair well with garlic, pork, cabbage, and potatoes. They can be used whole, ground, or toasted to release their aromatic oils, enhancing their flavor.

Medicinal Properties

Traditionally, caraway has been used for its digestive benefits. The seeds contain essential oils, including carvone and limonene, which can help to soothe the digestive tract, reduce gas, and alleviate cramping. Caraway is also recognized for its antispasmodic and carminative properties.

Cultural Significance

In various cultures, caraway seeds have been used not only in cooking but also in traditional medicine and as a symbol of protection and love. They are thought to ward off evil spirits and were traditionally included in wedding ceremonies and baked into bread as a symbol of fidelity.

Production

The leading producers of caraway are Finland, the Netherlands, and Poland, along with other countries in Europe and North Africa. The seeds are harvested in late summer, once the plant is mature and dry.

Other Facts

Caraway seeds are often confused with cumin and fennel seeds due to their similar appearance and flavor profile, but they are distinct in taste and culinary application. Caraway oil, extracted from the seeds, is used in the flavoring of mouthwashes, toothpaste, and cosmetics.

Cardamom

Cardamom, renowned for its aromatic seeds, is a highly valued spice in culinary traditions around the globe, particularly in Indian, Middle Eastern, and Scandinavian cuisines. Cardamom belongs to the ginger family, Zingiberaceae, and is native to the Indian subcontinent and Indonesia. It grows as a perennial herb with large, green leaves and bears small, pod-like fruits that contain the seeds. There are two main types of cardamom: green cardamom (Elettaria cardamomum) and black cardamom (Amomum subulatum), each with its unique flavor profile.

Culinary Uses

Cardamom's flavor is complex, sweet, spicy, and highly aromatic, making it a versatile spice for both sweet and savory dishes. Green cardamom, with its delicate and slightly sweet flavor, is used in desserts, pastries, and beverages like chai tea, as well as in savory dishes such as curries and rice dishes. Black cardamom has a smokier, more robust flavor and is typically used in heartier savory dishes, including stews and meat dishes. Cardamom pairs well with cinnamon, cloves, and nutmeg in spice blends and is a key ingredient in garam masala and Scandinavian baking.

Medicinal Properties

Traditionally, cardamom is believed to help with digestive issues, such as bloating and gas, and has been used in traditional medicine to treat sore throats and relieve symptoms of colds and flu.

Cultural Significance

Cardamom holds significant cultural importance in many societies. In South Asia, it is a symbol of hospitality and is often served in coffee or tea to welcome guests. In the Middle East, cardamom-flavored coffee is a traditional offering. In Scandinavian countries, cardamom is essential in baking, especially during the Christmas season.

Production

Guatemala is currently the largest producer of cardamom, followed by India and Sri Lanka The pods must be picked by hand when they are just ripe to ensure the highest quality.

Other Facts

Cardamom is one of the world's most expensive spices by weight, second only to saffron and vanilla, due to its labor-intensive harvesting process and the amount of work required to grow and process the pods. In addition to culinary uses, cardamom is also used in traditional medicine and perfumery.

Cardamom, black

Black Cardamom, known for its smoky, camphor-like flavor, is a distinct spice integral to various cuisines, particularly in South Asian and Middle Eastern dishes. Black Cardamom (Amomum subulatum) belongs to the ginger family, Zingiberaceae, and is native to the eastern Himalayas and subtropical regions of India, Nepal, and Bhutan. Unlike its cousin, green cardamom, black cardamom is larger in size with a tough, dark brown pod that encases the seeds.

Culinary Uses

Black Cardamom's flavor is robust and smoky, due to traditional drying over open flames, with notes of resin and camphor, and a cooling menthol undertone. It is primarily used in savory dishes, imparting depth to curries, stews, and rice dishes. In Indian cuisine, it is a key component of garam masala and other spice blends, essential for dishes like biryanis and kebabs. Its strong flavor complements red meats and hearty vegetables well. Unlike green cardamom, which finds its way into desserts and sweet dishes, black cardamom is almost exclusively used in savory recipes.

Medicinal Properties

Traditionally, black cardamom has been used in Ayurvedic medicine to treat respiratory conditions, such as asthma and bronchitis, due to its expectorant properties. The spice is thought to have antimicrobial and antioxidant properties as well.

Cultural Significance

While not as widely celebrated in cultural traditions as green cardamom, black cardamom holds a place in the culinary heritage of the regions where it is produced and used. Its distinctive flavor is associated with the warming, comforting dishes of winter and festive occasions in South Asian cultures.

Production

The main producers of black cardamom are India, Nepal, and Bhutan, where the climate and elevation are ideal for its growth.

Other Facts

Due to its powerful flavor, black cardamom is used more sparingly than green cardamom. It is an essential spice for anyone looking to explore the depth and complexity of South Asian cooking.

Cassia

Cassia, often referred to as Chinese cinnamon, is a widely used spice that comes from the bark of the Cinnamomum cassia plant, belonging to the Lauraceae family. Native to southern China and parts of Southeast Asia, cassia has been utilized both as a culinary ingredient and in traditional medicine for thousands of years. It is a close relative of true cinnamon (Cinnamomum verum), but it is characterized by a thicker, rougher bark and a stronger, more pungent flavor.

Culinary Uses

Cassia's flavor is robust, warm, and spicy, with a distinct sweetness and a hint of bitterness, making it a favored spice in various cuisines. It is commonly used in the preparation of savory dishes, desserts, and spice mixes, such as five-spice powder. Cassia is also a key ingredient in many curry powders and masala blends. In addition to its culinary applications, cassia is used to flavor beverages, including teas and liqueurs. Its bold flavor makes it suitable for dishes requiring a pronounced cinnamon taste, and it pairs well with cloves, nutmeg, and ginger.

Medicinal Properties

Traditionally, cassia has been valued in Chinese and Ayurvedic medicine for its health benefits, including its ability to improve digestion, reduce nausea, and treat colds and flu.

Cultural Significance

Cassia has a long history in both culinary and medicinal contexts across Asia. It has been traded along spice routes for centuries, contributing to its spread and integration into various regional cuisines and healing practices. Its warm, comforting aroma is associated with festive occasions, especial

Production

China, Indonesia, and Vietnam are the primary producers of cassia, where the climate is well-suited for the growth of Cinnamomum cassia trees. The bark is harvested during the rainy season when it is more pliable, then it is dried and rolled into scrolls or ground into powder.

Other Facts

Cassia is often sold as cinnamon in many parts of the world, leading to confusion between the two spices. While they are related and have similar uses, cassia is generally less expensive and has a more assertive flavor than true cinnamon.

Cayenne pepper

Cayenne pepper, known for its fiery heat and bright red color, is a staple spice in many global cuisines, adding both heat and depth to dishes. Derived from the dried pods of chili peppers, cayenne belongs to the Capsicum annuum species, part of the nightshade family, Solanaceae. Native to the tropical Americas, cayenne peppers have been cultivated and valued for thousands of years, spreading worldwide through trade and exploration. The ground spice is made from various types of hot chili peppers, sometimes labeled simply as "red pepper" or "hot pepper."

Culinary Uses

Cayenne pepper's flavor is intensely spicy with a subtle, earthy undertone, making it a popular ingredient in cuisines that favor heat, such as Mexican, Indian, Cajun, and Creole. It is used to season meats, seafood, sauces, and soups, and can also be found in spice blends, marinades, and rubs. Cayenne adds a significant kick to dishes without overshadowing other flavors, enhancing the overall complexity of a meal. It pairs well with ingredients like garlic, lime, and honey, balancing its heat with their flavors. Cayenne pepper is typically used in powdered form but can also be found as whole dried peppers or in hot sauce.

Medicinal Properties

Cayenne pepper is celebrated for its health benefits, primarily due to its active component, capsaicin. Capsaicin is known for its pain-relief properties, used in topical creams to alleviate joint and muscle pain. Additionally, cayenne has been associated with boosting metabolism, supporting cardiovascular health, and aiding digestion.

Cultural Significance

Cayenne pepper holds significant cultural importance in many regions, symbolizing strength and endurance. In traditional medicine, it has been used for its warming and circulatory benefits.

Production

Today, cayenne pepper is grown in many parts of the world, with India, China, and Mexico being major producers. The peppers are harvested, sun-dried, and then ground into a fine powder.

Other Facts

Cayenne pepper is rated between 30,000 to 50,000 Scoville Heat Units (SHU), indicating its level of spiciness. This heat level makes it moderately hot compared to other chili peppers.

Celery leaf

Celery leaf, often overlooked in favor of the more commonly used celery stalks, is a flavorful and aromatic herb that belongs to the Apiaceae family, the same family as carrots and parsley. Celery (Apium graveolens) is native to the Mediterranean region and has been cultivated for thousands of years for its medicinal properties and crisp, refreshing flavor. The leaves of the celery plant are dark green, with a delicate, lacy appearance and a flavor that is similar to the stalks but with a slightly stronger, herbaceous note.

Culinary Uses

Celery leaves are versatile in culinary applications, adding a fresh, slightly bitter, and peppery flavor to a variety of dishes. They can be used much like parsley or other leafy herbs, finely chopped as a garnish for soups, salads, and stews, or incorporated into sauces, dressings, and marinades. They pair well with garlic, onion, carrots, and potatoes, and can be used to enhance the flavor of chicken, fish, and vegetable dishes. To preserve their delicate flavor, celery leaves are best added towards the end of cooking or used fresh.

Medicinal Properties

Traditionally, celery leaves have been valued for their diuretic properties, aiding in the reduction of water retention and supporting kidney health. They are rich in vitamins and minerals, including Vitamin A, Vitamin C, and potassium, contributing to overall health and wellness.

Cultural Significance

While celery leaves do not have the same widespread cultural significance as some herbs and spices, they have been used in traditional medicine for centuries, particularly in their native Mediterranean and Middle Eastern regions.

Production

Celery is cultivated worldwide, with major producers including the United States, Mexico, and parts of Europe.. Celery leaves are harvested along with the stalks, but are often discarded or overlooked in favor of the more commonly consumed stalks.

Celery seed

Celery seed, derived from the plant Apium graveolens, is a versatile and potent spice used in various global cuisines. Belonging to the Apiaceae family, the same family as carrots and parsley, celery is native to the Mediterranean region and the Middle East. While the plant is widely known for its crisp stalks and flavorful leaves, the seeds – small, brown, and round – are packed with flavor and have been used both culinarily and medicinally for centuries.

Culinary Uses

Celery seed's flavor is strong and somewhat bitter, with a distinct celery-like taste and slightly earthy undertones. It is used to enhance the flavors of soups, stews, salads, and pickling recipes. Celery seed is a key ingredient in coleslaw and potato salad, where its pungent taste can stand up to creamy dressings. It also features prominently in spice blends, such as Old Bay seasoning, and is used to season meats and vegetable dishes.

Medicinal Properties

Historically, celery seed has been used for its diuretic properties, aiding in the removal of excess water from the body. It is also believed to have anti-inflammatory and antioxidant benefits, potentially helping to reduce blood pressure and combat infections.

Cultural Significance

While not as culturally symbolic as some herbs and spices, celery seed has been recognized in traditional medicine, especially within Ayurvedic practices, for its ability to treat a variety of ailments, from colds to arthritis. Its use in cooking spans many cultures, reflecting its adaptability and the depth it can add to a wide range of dishes.

Production

Celery seed is harvested from the mature plant once the flowers have bloomed and the seeds begin to turn brown. India, China, and Europe are notable producers, utilizing both wild and cultivated forms of the celery plant.

Other Facts

In addition to culinary and medicinal uses, celery seed is also used in the food industry as a flavoring agent in condiments, such as salad dressings and sauces. Due to its concentrated flavor, it is advisable to use celery seed sparingly in cooking.

Chervil

Chervil, known for its delicate leaves and subtle flavor, is a cherished herb in French cuisine, particularly as a component of the classic "fines herbes" blend alongside parsley, tarragon, and chives. Chervil (Anthriscus cerefolium) belongs to the Apiaceae family, sharing its lineage with parsley, carrots, and dill. It is native to Eastern Europe and parts of Asia but has been widely adopted in kitchens across Europe and North America. Chervil is an annual herb, characterized by its light green, lacy leaves and small, white flowers, reminiscent of its close relative, parsley, but with a more refined taste.

Culinary Uses

Chervil's flavor is mild and slightly anise-like, with hints of licorice and parsley. It is commonly used in soups, salads, egg dishes, and sauces, where its subtle taste can complement without overpowering other ingredients. Chervil is a key ingredient in béarnaise sauce, a staple of French cuisine. Its delicate nature means it should be added towards the end of cooking or used fresh to preserve its flavor and vibrant color. Chervil pairs well with fish, poultry, young vegetables, and is excellent in herb butters and soft cheeses.

Medicinal Properties

Traditionally, chervil has been used for its mild digestive and diuretic properties. It is believed to help lower blood pressure and promote digestion. Like many leafy greens, chervil is a source of vitamins and minerals, including vitamin C, calcium, and iron, contributing to its health benefits.

Cultural Significance

In French culinary tradition, chervil is not just an herb but a symbol of refined taste, embodying the subtlety and finesse of French cuisine. It is celebrated in the spring, often used in dishes that mark the renewal of the season. Chervil's delicate flavor and appearance have also made it a popular choice for garnishing and enhancing the presentation of dishes.

Production

Chervil thrives in cool, moist conditions and is often found in temperate regions. It can be more challenging to grow than other herbs due to its preference for shade and moisture, which makes it less commonly available in markets than more robust herbs.

Chicory

Chicory, known for its bitter flavor and versatile use, is a perennial herb belonging to the dandelion family, Asteraceae. Native to Europe, it has been naturalized in North America and other parts of the world. Chicory (Cichorium intybus) is characterized by its bright blue flowers, woody stem, and large leaves. The plant is cultivated for its leaves, buds, and roots, each part serving different culinary and medicinal purposes.

Culinary Uses

Chicory's leaves, often called endive or radicchio, vary in taste from bitter to mildly sweet and are used in salads, sautéed dishes, or as a cooked green. The roots are perhaps the most distinct part of the plant; when roasted and ground, they are used as a coffee substitute or additive, especially in New Orleans' famous chicory coffee. This coffee blend is known for its rich, slightly bitter flavor, offering a caffeine-free alternative with a depth similar to regular coffee. Chicory root is also a source of inulin, a type of prebiotic fiber, and is used in health foods and as a dietary supplement.

Medicinal Properties

Traditionally, chicory has been used for its digestive benefits, attributed to its high inulin content, which supports gut health and promotes the growth of beneficial bacteria. It has also been used to treat liver and gallbladder disorders, reduce inflammation, and manage diabetes due to its potential to regulate blood sugar levels.

Cultural Significance

Chicory has a long history of use in folk medicine and as a food source. Its adoption in coffee blends, particularly during times of coffee scarcity, has cemented its place in certain culinary traditions, notably in France and New Orleans. The plant's ability to grow in poor conditions has also made it a symbol of resilience and adaptability.

Production

While chicory is native to Europe, its cultivation has spread worldwide, with major producers including France, Belgium, and the United States. The cultivation process varies depending on the part of the plant being harvested. Leaves may be grown for salad greens, while roots are cultivated more like root vegetables, harvested in the fall when their inulin content is highest.

Chili pepper

Chili pepper, renowned for its heat and flavor, is a pivotal ingredient in cuisines around the globe, from the Americas to Asia. Belonging to the genus Capsicum, chili peppers are part of the nightshade family, Solanaceae, which also includes tomatoes and potatoes. Native to the Americas, chili peppers have been cultivated and cherished for thousands of years, with their seeds spread worldwide through trade and exploration. There are numerous varieties of chili peppers, ranging from the mild bell pepper to the fiery Carolina Reaper, each with its unique flavor profile and heat level.

Culinary Uses

The flavor of chili peppers is complex and varies widely among types, from mildly sweet to intensely hot, often with fruity or smoky undertones. They are a staple in many types of cuisine, such as Mexican, Indian, Thai, and Korean, used to add heat and depth to dishes including salsas, curries, stews, and sauces. Chili peppers can be used fresh, dried, powdered (as in paprika), or as a paste, and are integral to spice blends such as curry powders and chili powders. They pair well with a variety of ingredients, enhancing flavors and adding a spicy kick to meats, vegetables, and even some desserts.

Medicinal Properties

Chili peppers are celebrated for their health benefits, largely attributed to capsaicin, the compound that gives them their heat. Capsaicin has been shown to have analgesic properties, providing pain relief for conditions such as arthritis and neuropathy.

Cultural Significance

Chili peppers hold significant cultural importance in many societies, symbolizing strength, purity, and passion. Today, chili peppers are celebrated in festivals and culinary competitions around the world, showcasing their versatility and integral role in cultural identity and cuisine.

Production

Originally cultivated in regions of Central and South America, chili peppers are now grown worldwide, with major producers including China, Turkey, Nigeria, and Mexico. The cultivation of chili peppers varies with climate, species, and desired use, ranging from small-scale backyard gardens to large agricultural operations. The peppers are harvested at various stages of maturity, depending on the intended use, with some varieties picked while still green and others left on the plant to ripen and develop more intense heat and flavor.

Chironji

Chironji, also known as Charoli, is a lesser-known but highly valued spice and nut in Indian cuisine, derived from the seeds of Buchanania lanzan, a deciduous tree native to India and parts of Southeast Asia. Belonging to the family Anacardiaceae, chironji plays a dual role in culinary and medicinal contexts, akin to almonds and pine nuts in other cultures. The tree is characterized by its straight trunk, lance-shaped leaves, and small, fleshy fruits, inside which the edible seeds are encased.

Culinary Uses

Chironji seeds have a delicate and slightly sweet flavor, making them a popular ingredient in Indian sweets and desserts, such as kheer, barfi, and halwa. They are also used as a thickening agent in savory dishes and gravies, contributing a nutty texture and flavor similar to almonds. Chironji can be used whole or ground into a powder and is often toasted to enhance its taste. Its subtle, aromatic flavor pairs well with dairy-based dishes, enhancing the richness of the cuisine.

Medicinal Properties

Traditionally, chironji has been valued in Ayurvedic medicine for its cooling properties and is used to treat a variety of ailments, including skin rashes, blemishes, and digestive issues. The seeds are rich in vitamins and minerals, such as vitamin C, vitamin B1, iron, and calcium, contributing to their health benefits. They are believed to have antioxidant properties, aiding in the detoxification of the body and promoting skin health.

Cultural Significance

In India, chironji holds a place of culinary and medicinal importance, often featured in festive foods and traditional remedies. Its use in royal and traditional cuisines reflects its status as a luxury ingredient, cherished for its unique flavor and health benefits.

Production

Chironji is primarily harvested in the wild forests of India, making it a relatively rare and expensive ingredient compared to more commonly available nuts and seeds. The seeds are collected from the fruit of the Buchanania lanzan tree, which is manually cracked open to extract the edible seeds. The labor-intensive process of harvesting and preparing chironji seeds contributes to their higher price.

Chives

Chives, known for their delicate flavor and vibrant green color, are a common herb in culinary traditions around the world. Chives (Allium schoenoprasum) belong to the Amaryllidaceae family, closely related to garlic, onions, leeks, and scallions. Native to Europe, Asia, and North America, chives are a perennial plant, characterized by their thin, tube-shaped leaves and edible purple flowers. They are easy to grow in temperate climates, flourishing in both gardens and pots.

Culinary Uses

Chives' flavor is mild and subtly onion-like, making them a perfect addition to a wide range of dishes. They are commonly used fresh as a garnish on soups, salads, omelets, and baked potatoes. Chives also enhance the taste of dips, dressings, and butter, adding a hint of onion without overpowering other flavors. The flowers, apart from being decorative, are edible and can be used in salads for a mild, slightly garlicky taste. Chives are best added towards the end of cooking or used raw to preserve their delicate flavor and bright color. They pair well with cream-based sauces, eggs, potatoes, and fish.

Medicinal Properties

Traditionally, chives have been used for their medicinal properties, including their ability to aid digestion and boost the immune system. They are rich in vitamins A and C, antioxidants, and minerals such as potassium and iron. Chives also have mild anti-inflammatory properties and can help reduce the risk of certain diseases due to their nutrient content.

Cultural Significance

While chives may not hold the symbolic importance of some herbs, they have been used in cooking for centuries and are valued for their culinary versatility. In various cultures, chives are appreciated for their ease of cultivation and the subtle enhancement they bring to dishes.

Production

Chives are widely cultivated and can be found fresh in supermarkets throughout the year. They are harvested by cutting the leaves close to the base, encouraging the plant to produce new growth. Chives are best when used fresh but can also be frozen or dried, although drying may result in a loss of flavor.

Cicely

Sweet Cicely, known for its sweet, anise-flavored leaves, is a valued herb in culinary and medicinal practices, particularly in European traditions. Sweet Cicely (Myrrhis odorata) belongs to the Apiaceae family, which includes carrots, parsley, and dill. It is native to parts of Europe and Asia and is characterized by its fern-like, aromatic leaves, and white, umbel-shaped flowers. Sweet Cicely is a perennial herb, thriving in temperate climates and woodland settings.

Culinary Uses

Sweet Cicely's flavor is distinctly sweet and reminiscent of anise or licorice, making it a unique addition to both sweet and savory dishes. It can be used to sweeten tart fruits like rhubarb and reduce the amount of sugar needed in recipes. The leaves are often added to salads, soups, and stews for a hint of sweetness and aroma. Sweet Cicely seeds, which also carry the plant's characteristic anise flavor, can be used as a spice or garnish. In addition to its leaves and seeds, the root of Sweet Cicely can be cooked similarly to a vegetable, offering a sweet, aromatic taste.

Medicinal Properties

Traditionally, Sweet Cicely has been used for a variety of medicinal purposes. It is believed to have digestive benefits, helping to relieve gas and indigestion. The herb has also been used as an expectorant to treat coughs and as a gentle tonic for general health. Its antiseptic properties make it useful in herbal remedies for cuts and wounds.

Cultural Significance

While Sweet Cicely may not be as widely recognized in modern culinary arts as some herbs, it holds a place in traditional European cooking and herbal medicine. It was historically valued for its sweetening properties, especially before the widespread availability of sugar, and was used to make medicines more palatable.

Production

Sweet Cicely is not as commonly cultivated on a large scale as other herbs, but it can be found in herb gardens and specialty markets. It prefers shaded areas and rich, moist soil, making it suitable for woodland gardens or shaded garden corners. The plant is propagated from seed or by dividing established plants in spring or autumn.

Cilantro (coriander)

Cilantro, also known as coriander or Chinese parsley, is an essential herb in global cuisines, particularly in Latin American, Indian, and Southeast Asian dishes. Cilantro (Coriandrum sativum) belongs to the Apiaceae family, which includes carrots, celery, and parsley. It is native to regions spanning Southern Europe, Northern Africa, and Southwestern Asia. Cilantro is an annual herb, recognized by its bright green, fan-shaped leaves, and is unique in that both its leaves and seeds (coriander seeds) are used in cooking, offering two distinct flavors.

Culinary Uses

Cilantro's flavor is fresh and citrusy, with a polarizing effect; some people adore it, while others find it tastes like soap due to a genetic trait. It is a key ingredient in salsa, guacamole, chutneys, and as a garnish for soups and curries. The herb pairs well with lime, tomatoes, beans, and meats. Coriander seeds, on the other hand, have a warm, spicy, and citrusy flavor, used ground or whole in spice mixes, marinades, and as a seasoning for meat and vegetable dishes. Cilantro is best added at the end of cooking or used raw to preserve its delicate flavor and vibrant color.

Medicinal Properties

Cilantro has been used for its digestive and anti-inflammatory properties. It is rich in antioxidants and vitamins A, C, and K. It is also believed to have antimicrobial properties and may help in lowering blood sugar levels.

Cultural Significance

Cilantro holds a significant place in many cultures, used not only for its culinary attributes but also in traditional medicines. In India, it is a staple in spice blends and Ayurvedic remedies. In Latin America, it is indispensable in the daily diet, used in a variety of dishes for its fresh, tangy flavor.

Production

Cilantro is cultivated worldwide, with major production in countries such as India, China, and Mexico. It thrives in cooler climates but can be grown in a wide range of environments. The herb is harvested for its leaves, while coriander seeds are collected when the plant matures and the seeds dry on the plant.

Other Facts

Cilantro is known for its rapid growth cycle and tendency to bolt in hot conditions, which makes continuous sowing a good practice for a steady supply.

Cinnamon

Cinnamon, renowned for its warm, sweet aroma and flavor, is a staple spice in both sweet and savory dishes across the globe. Derived from the inner bark of trees belonging to the genus Cinnamomum, cinnamon is native to Sri Lanka, Bangladesh, India, and Myanmar, with Cinnamomum verum (Ceylon cinnamon) and Cinnamomum cassia (Cassia cinnamon) being the most common types. Cinnamon has been traded and cherished for millennia, both for its culinary uses and medicinal properties.

Culinary Uses

Cinnamon's sweet, woody flavor is essential in a variety of dishes, from cinnamon rolls and pastries to curries and stews. It is a key ingredient in spice blends such as garam masala, Chinese five-spice, and pumpkin pie spice. Cinnamon enhances the taste of fruits, chocolates, and beverages like tea, coffee, and mulled wine. In savory dishes, it adds depth and warmth, pairing well with meats, curries, and marinades. The spice can be used in stick form, which is ideal for infusing flavors into liquids and sauces, or ground, for a more direct addition of flavor to recipes.

Medicinal Properties

Traditionally, cinnamon has been used for its health benefits, including digestive support, anti-inflammatory properties, and blood sugar regulation. It contains cinnamaldehyde, an active compound that is thought to have antioxidant and antimicrobial effects, potentially reducing the risk of heart disease and supporting metabolic health. Cinnamon is also known for its potential to improve insulin sensitivity and lower blood sugar levels, making it a beneficial spice for people with diabetes.

Cultural Significance

Cinnamon holds a significant place in many cultures, symbolizing prosperity, health, and warmth. It has been used in religious ceremonies, as a preservative, and as a luxury item traded along spice routes. The spice's rich history and exotic origin have made it a valuable and sought-after commodity throughout the ages.

Production

Sri Lanka is the largest producer of Ceylon cinnamon, while Indonesia, China, and Vietnam are the main producers of Cassia cinnamon. The harvesting process involves removing the tree bark and then scraping off the inner bark, which curls into quills as it dries. These quills are then cut into sticks or ground into powder.

Cinnamon myrtle

Cinnamon Myrtle, known for its warm, spicy aroma reminiscent of true cinnamon, is a unique herb native to Australia. Cinnamon Myrtle (Backhousia myrtifolia) is part of the Myrtaceae family, which includes other aromatic plants like clove and eucalyptus. It is a medium-sized rainforest tree characterized by its creamy white flowers and aromatic leaves. Unlike traditional cinnamon derived from tree bark, Cinnamon Myrtle's flavor comes from its leaves, making it a sustainable and versatile culinary herb.

Culinary Uses

Cinnamon Myrtle's leaves impart a sweet, cinnamon-like flavor, making them suitable for a wide range of culinary applications. The leaves can be used fresh or dried and ground into a powder, adding depth to desserts, baked goods, teas, and spice rubs. It is particularly popular in creating uniquely Australian cuisine, where it flavors sauces, syrups, and even savory dishes such as curries and stews. Its compatibility with chocolate, fruits, and meats showcases its versatility in the kitchen. Cinnamon Myrtle is also celebrated in the beverage industry, where it flavors teas, cocktails, and infused waters.

Medicinal Properties

Traditionally, Cinnamon Myrtle has been used in Aboriginal Australian medicine for treating gastrointestinal issues and as an antiseptic. Modern herbalists value it for its essential oils, which possess antimicrobial and anti-inflammatory properties.

Cultural Significance

Cinnamon Myrtle holds a place in Australian botanical and culinary heritage, embodying the rich biodiversity of the continent's rainforest regions. Its use in contemporary Australian cuisine reflects a growing appreciation for native herbs and spices that offer unique flavors and health benefits.

Production

Cinnamon Myrtle is primarily cultivated in Australia, thriving in subtropical rainforest climates. It is grown both for its culinary appeal and ornamental value, with its attractive foliage and flowers. The cultivation and harvesting of Cinnamon Myrtle are sustainable, focusing on leaf production without harming the parent trees.

Clary

Clary Sage, often referred to simply as clary, is a valued herb known for its aromatic leaves and medicinal properties. Clary Sage (Salvia sclarea) belongs to the mint family, Lamiaceae, and is native to the Northern Mediterranean Basin, along with parts of North Africa and Central Asia. It is a biennial or short-lived perennial plant, characterized by its large, hairy leaves and tall spikes of flowers, which range in color from pale lavender to white.

Culinary Uses

While not as commonly used in cooking as other herbs, clary sage leaves can be used in small amounts to flavor certain dishes. Its leaves have a slightly nutty, balsamic taste that pairs well with savory dishes. The herb is occasionally used to impart flavor to wines and liqueurs, as well as in some herbal teas for its aromatic properties. However, due to its potent flavor, it is used sparingly in culinary applications.

Medicinal Properties

Clary sage is highly regarded for its medicinal benefits. It contains essential oils that have been used in traditional medicine to treat a variety of ailments. The herb is known for its calming and sedative effects, making it useful for treating anxiety and insomnia. It is also used for digestive problems, as it can help to relieve indigestion and stomach cramps. Additionally, clary sage is sometimes used in women's health for its purported benefits in relieving menstrual pain and regulating cycles.

Cultural Significance

In traditional practices, clary sage was often used in eye health, with the seeds being used to remove particles from the eyes, which is how it got its name "clary" from "clear eye." While it does not hold a prominent place in culinary traditions, its use in aromatherapy and natural medicine has given it a significant role in wellness cultures.

Production

Clary sage is cultivated in regions that mimic its native climate, including parts of Europe and North America. It is grown for its essential oil, which is extracted from the flowers and leaves and used in perfumery, aromatherapy, and natural medicine. The plant prefers full sun and well-drained soil and is harvested when the flowers are in full bloom to maximize oil yield.

Clove

Clove, known for its intense aroma and pungent, sweet flavor, is a staple spice in cuisines and traditional medicine worldwide. Clove (Syzygium aromaticum) is part of the Myrtaceae family and is native to the Maluku Islands in Indonesia. It is harvested from the flower buds of the clove tree, which are picked by hand and then dried until they turn a deep brown color. Cloves are used whole or ground and have a very strong, spicy flavor that is warm and slightly numbing.

Culinary Uses

Clove's rich, warm flavor is key in a variety of dishes across many cultures. It is a crucial ingredient in spice blends such as Chinese five-spice, Indian garam masala, and Middle Eastern baharat. In baking, cloves are often used in spice mixes for cookies, cakes, and other desserts, especially during the holiday season. Cloves also flavor savory dishes, including stews, marinades, and meat dishes, and are used to stud hams and pork, imparting a distinctive taste. In beverages, cloves are found in mulled wines, ciders, and teas, adding depth and warmth.

Medicinal Properties

Traditionally, cloves have been used for their antiseptic, analgesic, and anti-inflammatory properties. The spice contains eugenol, a compound that can help to relieve pain, especially toothaches, and reduce inflammation. Cloves are also believed to aid digestion, combat nausea, and have antimicrobial properties that can help fight infections.

Cultural Significance

Cloves have a long history of use in both culinary and medicinal contexts, dating back thousands of years. They were highly valued in ancient Rome and China, not only as a spice but also for their medicinal properties. In the Middle Ages, cloves became part of the lucrative spice trade, symbolizing wealth and status in Europe. They continue to be an essential element in religious and cultural ceremonies in various parts of the world.

Production

Today, cloves are cultivated in tropical climates around the world, with Indonesia, Madagascar, Zanzibar, and Sri Lanka among the leading producers. The cultivation and harvest of cloves are labor-intensive processes, as the buds must be picked at just the right time and carefully dried to preserve their flavor and aromatic properties.

Coriander seed

Coriander seed, derived from the Coriandrum sativum plant, is a versatile spice that plays a central role in cuisines across the globe, including Latin American, Middle Eastern, Indian, and Southeast Asian dishes. Unlike cilantro, which refers to the fresh leaves of the same plant, coriander seeds offer a vastly different flavor profile. The seeds are part of the Apiaceae family, which also includes celery, carrots, and parsley. Native to the Mediterranean and Middle Eastern regions, coriander has been cultivated and used in cooking and as a medicinal herb for thousands of years.

Culinary Uses

Coriander seeds possess a sweet, earthy, and citrusy flavor, making them a beloved spice in a wide range of culinary applications. They are used whole or ground into powder and are a key ingredient in spice blends such as garam masala, curry powder, and ras el hanout. Coriander seeds are also used to flavor soups, stews, pickles, and baked goods, and they complement meat and vegetable dishes. In brewing, coriander seeds are often added to certain styles of beer, such as Belgian witbiers, for their aromatic qualities. The spice pairs well with cumin, turmeric, ginger, and chili.

Medicinal Properties

Traditionally, coriander seeds have been valued for their medicinal properties, including their ability to aid digestion, relieve gas, and reduce inflammation. They are also believed to have antimicrobial and antifungal effects. The seeds are a source of dietary fiber, vitamins, and minerals like iron, magnesium, and manganese, contributing to their health benefits.

Cultural Significance

Coriander seeds have a rich history and have been found in ancient archaeological sites, including tombs of the pharaohs in Egypt, signifying their long-standing value and use. In various cultures, coriander seeds have been used not only in cooking but also in traditional healing practices and ceremonies.

Production

Today, coriander seeds are cultivated in countries around the world, with major producers including India, Morocco, Canada, Russia, and parts of Europe. The plant prefers a mild climate and well-drained soil. It is harvested when the seeds turn brown and are dried before being threshed to collect the seeds.

Coriander, Vietnamese

Vietnamese Coriander, also known as Rau Răm or Vietnamese Cilantro, is a pivotal herb in Southeast Asian cuisine, especially within Vietnamese dishes. Unlike Coriandrum sativum, which is known for its seeds (coriander) and leaves (cilantro), Vietnamese Coriander (Persicaria odorata) belongs to the Polygonaceae family. It is a perennial herb that thrives in tropical and subtropical regions, characterized by its long, narrow leaves, which are dark green with a unique burgundy pattern.

Culinary Uses

Vietnamese Coriander's flavor is a distinctive blend of spicy, tangy, and slightly peppery with a hint of lemon. This makes it an essential ingredient in Vietnamese cooking, used in salads, soups, spring rolls, and as a garnish for various meat and noodle dishes. It is particularly favored in dishes like phở and bánh xèo for its ability to add depth and freshness. The herb is used fresh, often added at the end of cooking or used as a raw garnish to preserve its vibrant flavor and aroma. It pairs well with mint, basil, and lime in culinary applications.

Medicinal Properties

Traditionally, Vietnamese Coriander has been used in Southeast Asian medicine to treat digestive issues, including stomachaches and indigestion. It is also believed to have antipyretic properties, used to reduce fever. Additionally, the herb is used for its antimicrobial and anti-inflammatory benefits, supporting wound healing and overall health.

Cultural Significance

Vietnamese Coriander holds significant cultural importance in Vietnamese cuisine, symbolizing the fresh, aromatic flavors that are characteristic of the region's dishes. Its use in traditional medicine underscores the herb's value beyond culinary applications, reflecting a holistic approach to health and wellness in Vietnamese culture.

Production

Vietnamese Coriander is cultivated in Southeast Asia and in warm, humid climates worldwide. It can be grown in water gardens or moist soil conditions, making it a versatile plant for culinary gardens. The herb prefers full sun to partial shade and requires regular watering to maintain its lush growth.

Costmary

Costmary, also known as Bible leaf or Alecost, is an old-fashioned herb that was once a staple in herb gardens but is less commonly found today. Costmary (Tanacetum balsamita) belongs to the Asteraceae family, which includes daisies and sunflowers. It is native to the Middle East and the Mediterranean region. Costmary is a perennial herb, characterized by its long, narrow leaves that have a sweet, balsamic fragrance, and small, yellow or white flowers that bloom in clusters.

Culinary Uses

Historically, Costmary leaves were used in cooking for their sweet, mildly minty flavor. They were added to salads, soups, and stews, and used to flavor ale and other beverages. The leaves could also be baked into cakes and biscuits for their aromatic quality. However, due to its strong flavor, Costmary is used sparingly in modern cuisine. The leaves are sometimes candied as a decorative and edible garnish for desserts.

Medicinal Properties

Traditionally, Costmary was valued for its medicinal properties. The herb was also known for its ability to relieve headaches and muscular pain. In historical contexts, Costmary leaves were often placed in Bibles as bookmarks, believed to offer a refreshing scent and possibly to ward off pests.

Cultural Significance

Costmary holds a place in historical herb gardens and has been used since ancient times in various cultures for its aromatic and medicinal qualities. Its common name, "Bible leaf," reflects its historical use as a natural bookmark in Bibles, where its scent would help to keep the pages fresh and possibly deter insects.

Production

Costmary is easy to grow in temperate climates and can be cultivated in herb gardens or as a decorative plant in borders and flower beds. It prefers full sun to partial shade and well-drained soil. The plant is propagated through division or cuttings, as it rarely produces viable seeds. Costmary is harvested by picking the leaves as needed, preferably in the morning when the aromatic oils are most concentrated.

Other Facts

Costmary's use has declined over time, and it is now more commonly grown as an ornamental plant or for historical interest in herb gardens.

Cubeb pepper

Cubeb pepper, known for its distinctive flavor and medicinal properties, is a spice that hails from the Piperaceae family, the same family as black and white pepper. Cubeb (Piper cubeba) is native to Indonesia and parts of Africa and is characterized by its small, round shape and the stem attached to the berry, which gives it the nickname "tailed pepper."

Culinary Uses

Cubeb pepper's flavor is pungent and slightly bitter, with a warm, eucalyptus-like aroma and a hint of allspice. It is used in Indonesian, North African, and Middle Eastern cuisines, adding depth to spice blends, meats, sauces, and spirits. Cubeb is particularly favored in Moroccan cooking, where it is a component of the spice mix Ras el Hanout. The spice has also historically been used in European medieval cuisine and is experiencing a resurgence among chefs and food enthusiasts looking for unique flavor profiles. Cubeb can be used whole or ground, though grinding it fresh before use is recommended to preserve its aromatic qualities.

Medicinal Properties

Traditionally, cubeb pepper has been used for its antiseptic, diuretic, and anti-inflammatory properties. It has been employed in herbal medicine to treat urinary tract infections, sore throat, and as a remedy for digestive issues. The spice is also believed to have aphrodisiac qualities and was used in various traditional medicines for this purpose.

Cultural Significance

Cubeb pepper was well-known in ancient and medieval times, traded along spice routes to Europe and the Middle East. It was highly valued for both its culinary and medicinal uses. However, its popularity in Europe declined with the advent of other spices. Today, cubeb is gaining interest again as chefs and home cooks explore historical cuisines and look for unique flavors to incorporate into modern dishes.

Production

The primary producer of cubeb pepper is Indonesia, where it grows as a vine in the tropical climate. The berries are harvested before they are fully ripe, then dried, which causes them to shrivel and retain the stem, distinguishing them from black pepper.

Culantro

Culantro, often confused with cilantro due to its similar aroma and flavor, is a distinct herb widely used in Caribbean, Latin American, and Southeast Asian cuisines. Culantro (Eryngium foetidum) belongs to the Apiaceae family, unlike cilantro which is part of the Coriandrum genus. It is native to the tropical regions of the Americas and is characterized by its long, serrated leaves that grow in a rosette pattern. Culantro is a biennial herb in tropical conditions but is often grown as an annual in temperate climates.

Culinary Uses

Culantro's flavor is more potent and enduring than that of cilantro, making it suitable for cooking processes that involve long simmering times. It is a staple ingredient in dishes such as sofrito, salsas, curries, stews, and marinades, where it imparts a deep, herbaceous aroma. The leaves are also used fresh in salads and as a garnish. In Southeast Asian cuisine, culantro complements spicy dishes with its cooling effect. Due to its strong flavor, culantro is used sparingly in culinary applications.

Medicinal Properties

Traditionally, culantro has been used for its medicinal properties, including as a remedy for colds, flu, diabetes, constipation, and fevers. It is believed to have anti-inflammatory and analgesic properties, making it useful in the treatment of headaches and high blood pressure. The herb is also thought to possess antibacterial qualities.

Cultural Significance

Culantro holds cultural importance in the regions where it is commonly used, often associated with traditional cooking methods and recipes passed down through generations. In the Caribbean, it is an indispensable herb in the creation of authentic local dishes, symbolizing the region's rich culinary heritage.

Production

Culantro thrives in hot, moist conditions, and its cultivation is most successful in partial shade, mimicking its natural under-canopy habitat. While not as widely available in supermarkets as cilantro, culantro can often be found in specialty ethnic stores or grown in home gardens. The herb is harvested by cutting the outer leaves, allowing the plant to continue producing foliage.

Cumin

Cumin, known for its distinctive earthy, slightly bitter flavor and warm aroma, is a staple spice in many global cuisines, most notably in Indian, Middle Eastern, and Latin American dishes. Cumin (Cuminum cyminum) belongs to the Apiaceae family, which includes parsley, carrots, and celery. It is native to the Eastern Mediterranean to India. Cumin is an annual herb, characterized by its slender, feathery leaves and small pink or white flowers. The spice is derived from the plant's dried, small, oblong seeds.

Culinary Uses

Cumin's flavor is unmistakable, marked by a nutty, peppery warmth that is essential in a variety of savory dishes. It is a key ingredient in spice blends such as garam masala, taco seasoning, and curry powders. Cumin seeds are used whole or ground and are often toasted before grinding to intensify their flavor. They are used to season meats, vegetables, soups, stews, and legumes. Cumin pairs well with coriander, chili, and other aromatic spices. In addition to its use in spice blends, cumin is also popular for flavoring breads and cheeses.

Medicinal Properties

Traditionally, cumin has been used for its digestive benefits, helping to stimulate the appetite and alleviate digestive issues such as bloating and gas. It is also known for its antioxidant properties and has been studied for its potential to improve blood sugar control and reduce cholesterol levels. Cumin contains several essential minerals, including iron, which is important for energy production and immune system function.

Cultural Significance

Cumin has a long history of use in culinary and medicinal practices, dating back to ancient civilizations. It was valued both for its flavor and its health benefits in ancient Egypt, Greece, and Rome. Today, cumin is celebrated in cuisines around the world for its distinctive taste that enriches a wide array of dishes.

Production

Cumin is cultivated in hot, tropical climates, with India being the largest producer, followed by other countries such as Iran, Turkey, and China. The plant requires a long, hot growing season to thrive. The seeds are harvested by hand after the plant flowers and then dried for use.

Curry leaf

Curry leaf, known for its distinctive aroma and flavor, is an essential herb in South Indian and Sri Lankan cuisines. Curry leaf (Murraya koenigii) belongs to the Rutaceae family, which also includes citrus fruits. It is native to the Indian subcontinent and is a tropical to subtropical tree characterized by its small, shiny green leaves that are highly aromatic.

Culinary Uses

Curry leaf's flavor is unique, offering a pungent and slightly bitter taste with notes of citrus. It is an indispensable ingredient in many South Indian dishes, such as curries, dals, and chutneys, imparting a depth of flavor that cannot be replicated by any other herb. The leaves are used whole or chopped and are typically fried in oil at the beginning of cooking to release their maximum flavor. Curry leaves are also used in marinades for meat and fish, adding a subtle but complex aroma. They pair well with mustard seeds, cumin, and turmeric in culinary applications.

Medicinal Properties

Traditionally, curry leaves have been used for their health benefits, including aiding digestion, promoting hair growth, and supporting liver health. They are rich in antioxidants and contain compounds that have been shown to have anti-diabetic properties. Curry leaves are also believed to have cholesterol-lowering effects and are used in traditional medicine to treat various ailments.

Cultural Significance

Curry leaves hold a significant place in Indian and Sri Lankan culinary traditions, regarded not only for their flavor but also for their health benefits. They are a symbol of flavor and aroma in South Indian cuisine and are indispensable in the region's cooking.

Production

Curry leaf trees are widely cultivated in tropical and subtropical regions of the Indian subcontinent, Australia, and Nigeria. The tree thrives in well-drained soils in full sun and is harvested for its leaves, which can be used fresh or dried. Fresh leaves are preferred for their superior flavor and aroma.

Cyperus articulates

Cyperus articulatus, commonly known as jointed flatsedge or piri piri, is a perennial herb native to tropical and subtropical regions of the Americas, Africa, and Asia. It belongs to the Cyperaceae family, closely related to sedges and rushes rather than true herbs. This plant is characterized by its tall, grass-like appearance, with jointed stems and narrow, lance-shaped leaves. The small, brownish flower heads are not particularly showy, but the plant is valued for its aromatic roots and rhizomes.

Culinary Uses

While not widely used in mainstream culinary practices, Cyperus articulatus has been utilized in traditional cooking in some cultures. Its aromatic roots are sometimes used to flavor beverages or as a spice in cooking, imparting a distinctive, earthy aroma. In some regions, it is added to teas and infusions for its flavor and medicinal properties.

Medicinal Properties

Cyperus articulatus is highly regarded in traditional medicine across various cultures for its wide range of health benefits. The plant's roots and rhizomes are believed to possess anti-inflammatory, diuretic, and antipyretic properties. It has been used to treat digestive issues, fevers, and urinary tract infections, as well as to alleviate pain and anxiety. The essential oils extracted from the roots are used in aromatherapy and herbal remedies.

Cultural Significance

In traditional societies, Cyperus articulatus has been used not only for its medicinal and aromatic qualities but also in spiritual practices. It is sometimes employed in rituals and ceremonies for protection or purification. The plant holds a place in the traditional pharmacopeia of many indigenous cultures, reflecting its importance in holistic health and well-being.

Production

Cyperus articulatus thrives in moist, tropical environments and is often found near water bodies. It is harvested from the wild rather than cultivated on a large scale. Sustainable harvesting practices are important to maintain local populations of the plant, as it plays a role in traditional medicine and ecosystems.

Dill

Dill, known for its feathery green leaves and distinctive, slightly sweet flavor, is an essential herb in many cuisines, particularly in Eastern Europe, Scandinavia, and the Mediterranean. Dill (Anethum graveolens) belongs to the Apiaceae family, which also includes parsley, cumin, and caraway. It is native to the Mediterranean region and parts of Eastern Europe but has become widely cultivated around the world. Dill is an annual herb, recognized for its slender stems, delicate leaves, and umbrella-shaped clusters of yellow flowers.

Culinary Uses

Dill's flavor is fresh and aromatic, with hints of anise and celery. It is commonly used in pickling, as well as in salads, soups, sauces, and fish dishes. Dill is particularly famous for its role in flavoring cucumbers during the pickling process, resulting in the classic dill pickle. In Scandinavian and Eastern European cuisines, dill is a key ingredient in dishes such as gravlax (cured salmon), borscht, and various potato and egg recipes. The herb pairs well with lemon, garlic, and mustard, and is often added towards the end of cooking or used fresh to preserve its delicate flavor.

Medicinal Properties

Traditionally, dill has been used for its digestive benefits. It is known to help relieve intestinal gas, cramps, and indigestion. Dill contains compounds such as carvone and limonene, which have been shown to have antimicrobial and anti-inflammatory properties. It is also a source of vitamin C, manganese, and iron, contributing to its health benefits.

Cultural Significance

Dill has been used for culinary and medicinal purposes since ancient times, with references to its use in Greek and Roman cultures. It symbolizes vitality and protection in some cultures and is associated with traditional celebrations and ceremonies, particularly in Northern and Eastern Europe.

Production

Dill is cultivated worldwide, with major production in Europe, Asia, and North America. It thrives in temperate climates and is relatively easy to grow in home gardens or commercially. Dill is harvested for its leaves (dill weed) and seeds, both of which are used in cooking and for their medicinal properties.

Dill seed

Dill seed, known for its distinct aroma and flavor, is a versatile spice used in various cuisines worldwide. Dill (Anethum graveolens) belongs to the Apiaceae family, which also includes parsley, cumin, and bay leaf. It is native to the Mediterranean region and southwestern Asia. Dill is an annual herb, characterized by its slender stems, soft leaves, and delicate, yellow flowers. The plant produces small, flat seeds that are used as a spice. There are not many varieties of dill, but the overall characteristics of the plant and its uses remain consistent across different regions.

Culinary Uses

Dill seed has a slightly bitter, sharp flavor with a hint of aromatic freshness, often compared to a combination of fennel, anise, and celery. It is commonly used in pickling, where it adds its signature taste to cucumbers and other vegetables. Dill seed is also a key ingredient in many European and Asian dishes, including soups, stews, and sauces. It pairs well with fish, potatoes, and yogurt-based sauces. In addition to the seeds, dill weed (the feathery leaves) is used for its less intense, more herby flavor, particularly in salads, dips, and as a garnish.

Medicinal properties

Traditionally, dill has been used for its digestive and soothing properties. It is known to help with indigestion, flatulence, and colic. The seeds contain essential oils, including carvone, which can have a calming effect on the stomach and aid in digestion. Dill is also a source of vitamin C, magnesium, and iron, contributing to its health benefits.

Cultural Significance

Dill has been used for centuries, with evidence of its cultivation dating back to Roman times and possibly earlier. It holds cultural significance in many countries; for example, in Scandinavian and Eastern European cuisines, dill is a fundamental ingredient, essential for the traditional flavors of many dishes.

Production

Russia, India, and Egypt are among the leading producers of dill seed. It is cultivated in many parts of the world with a temperate climate. The plant prefers a well-drained soil with good sunlight. Dill is harvested for its seeds and leaves, with the seeds being dried and used whole or ground into a powder.

Elderflower

Elderflower, renowned for its delicate, floral flavor, is a cherished herb and spice derived from the flowers of the elder tree (Sambucus nigra), which is part of the Adoxaceae family. This plant is native to parts of Europe, North Africa, and Western and Central Asia. It is a deciduous shrub or small tree, characterized by its creamy-white flowers and dark, berry-like fruits. Elderflower is celebrated not only for its culinary applications but also for its medicinal benefits.

Culinary Uses

Elderflower's flavor is subtly sweet and floral, making it a popular ingredient in a variety of culinary creations. It is famously used to make elderflower cordial, a sweet, concentrated syrup that serves as a base for drinks, cocktails, and even desserts. Elderflower also lends its unique taste to jams, jellies, and soft drinks, and can be found in some baking recipes where its floral notes complement pastries and cakes. In addition to these uses, elderflower is occasionally infused into vinegars and oils to add a distinctive flavor to salads and marinades.

Medicinal Properties

Historically, elderflower is believed to help alleviate cold and flu symptoms, thanks to its antiviral properties and its ability to induce sweating, which can help reduce fever.

Cultural Significance

In some traditions, the elder tree is considered magical and protective, believed to ward off evil spirits. Elderflower has been used in ceremonial practices and is sometimes associated with good health and prosperity.

Production

The flowers are typically collected in late spring to early summer, when they are at their most fragrant. After harvesting, the flowers can be used fresh or dried for later use. Countries across Europe, including the United Kingdom, Germany, and Hungary, are known for their elderflower production, utilizing both wild and cultivated sources.

Other Facts

Elderflower is not only valued for its culinary and medicinal uses but also for its role in eco-friendly gardening practices, as the elder tree provides habitat and food for a wide range of insects and birds.

Epazote

Epazote, known for its distinctive, pungent aroma, is a crucial herb in Mexican and Central American cuisines. Epazote (Dysphania ambrosioides), previously classified under the genus Chenopodium, is part of the Amaranthaceae family. It is native to Southern Mexico, Central America, and South America. This annual or perennial plant is characterized by its pointed, dark green leaves and red or green stems. Epazote is unique not only for its culinary uses but also for its medicinal properties and cultural significance.

Culinary Uses

Epazote's flavor is complex, described as a combination of oregano, anise, citrus, and mint with a slightly bitter undertone. It is most commonly used in traditional Mexican dishes such as beans, soups, and moles to impart a distinct flavor and to help reduce the flatulence associated with consuming beans. The herb is also used in making quesadillas, enchiladas, and other dishes where its robust flavor can stand out. Epazote is best used fresh but can also be found dried; however, the drying process significantly diminishes its potent aroma and flavor.

Medicinal Properties

Traditionally, epazote has been valued for its vermifuge properties, meaning it has been used to expel intestinal parasites. Epazote contains terpenoids and flavonoids that contribute to its medicinal benefits, though it should be used cautiously as large doses can be toxic.

Cultural Significance

In its native regions, epazote has been a part of traditional medicine and cooking for centuries. It is deeply embedded in the culinary traditions of Mexico and Central America, where it is appreciated not only for its flavor but also for its ability to aid digestion. The plant has been traditionally used in rituals and as a medicinal herb by indigenous cultures.

Production

Epazote grows widely in its native habitat and has been naturalized in parts of the United States and Europe. It thrives in a variety of environments but prefers well-drained soils and full sun. The plant is often grown in home gardens and is sometimes found as a wild herb.

Other Facts

Epazote is known for its ability to deter insects and pests, making it a beneficial companion plant in gardens.

Fennel

Fennel, renowned for its crisp, aromatic qualities, is a versatile herb and spice integral to various global cuisines, notably Italian and Mediterranean. Fennel (Foeniculum vulgare) belongs to the Apiaceae family, sharing lineage with parsley, carrots, and dill. Native to the Mediterranean, it is now cultivated worldwide. Fennel is a perennial herb, distinguished by its feathery green leaves, yellow flowers, and bulbous stem. It is unique for its anise-like flavor, derived from all its parts, including the bulb, stalk, leaves, and seeds.

Culinary Uses

Fennel's flavor is sweet and mildly licorice-like, making it a popular ingredient in salads, soups, and fish dishes. The bulb, when sliced, adds a crisp, refreshing texture and flavor to salads and slaws. It is also roasted or sautéed, which caramelizes the sugars, enhancing its sweetness. Fennel seeds are potent and aromatic, used ground or whole in sausages, breads, and desserts. They are also a key ingredient in spice blends like Chinese five-spice powder and Indian panch phoron. Fennel pairs well with seafood, pork, and in pickles, imparting a distinctive flavor that is both sweet and earthy.

Medicinal Properties

Fennel has been traditionally valued for its digestive benefits. It is known to alleviate bloating, gas, and stomach cramps, thanks to its antispasmodic properties. Fennel seeds contain anethole, a compound that can help to soothe the digestive tract and improve absorption of nutrients.

Cultural Significance

Fennel was revered by the ancient Greeks and Romans for its medicinal properties and was associated with Dionysus, the god of wine and festivity. In medieval times, fennel was used to ward off evil spirits, and its seeds were consumed to suppress appetite during fasting periods.

Production

Fennel is cultivated in many parts of the world, with Italy, India, and China among the leading producers. The plant thrives in sunny, well-drained soils and is harvested for its bulbs, seeds, and leaves. The bulb is harvested in the fall, while the seeds are collected in late summer to early fall when the flower heads turn brown.

Other Facts

Fennel pollen, collected from the flowers, is considered a delicacy and used as a spice to impart intense flavor to dishes.

Fenugreek

Fenugreek, known for its unique aromatic seeds and leaves, is a versatile herb and spice used in various cuisines worldwide, particularly in Indian, Middle Eastern, and North African dishes. Fenugreek (Trigonella foenum-graecum) belongs to the Fabaceae family and is native to the Mediterranean region, South Europe, and Western Asia. It is an annual plant, characterized by its green leaves, small white flowers, and hard, yellowish-brown seeds. There are no specific varieties of fenugreek commonly distinguished in culinary or medicinal contexts, as it is primarily valued for its seeds and, to a lesser extent, its leaves.

Culinary Uses

Fenugreek seeds have a slightly bitter, nutty flavor reminiscent of maple syrup and are often used in spice blends, including curry powders, masalas, and berbere. They can be used whole or ground into a powder and are essential in the preparation of pickles, daals, and other lentil dishes. Fenugreek leaves, known as methi, have a slightly bitter and aromatic flavor and are used fresh or dried in cooking. They are commonly used in Indian curries, vegetable dishes, and flatbreads like methi paratha. Fenugreek pairs well with strong spices, meats, and root vegetables. It is also used to flavor artificial maple syrup and in some traditional teas and beverages for its health benefits.

Medicinal Properties

Fenugreek has been traditionally used for its medicinal properties, including aiding digestion, enhancing lactation in nursing mothers, and managing blood sugar levels. The seeds contain soluble fiber, which can help in the treatment of constipation and maintaining healthy cholesterol levels. Fenugreek also contains several phytochemicals, including saponins and flavonoids, which have been studied for their anti-inflammatory and antidiabetic properties.

Cultural Significance

Fenugreek holds cultural significance in many parts of the world. In traditional medicine, it has been used for its digestive and soothing properties. In some cultures, fenugreek seeds are considered auspicious and used in cooking during special occasions and festivals.

Production

India is the largest producer of fenugreek, followed by other countries in the Mediterranean region, North Africa, and the Middle East. The plant thrives in arid and semi-arid climates and is harvested for its leaves and seeds. The seeds are the most commercially valuable part of the plant and are used both in culinary applications and for extracting fenugreek oil.

Filé powder

Filé powder, known for its earthy and slightly savory flavor, is a distinctive spice used primarily in Cajun and Creole cooking in the Southern United States. It is made from the dried and ground leaves of the sassafras tree (Sassafras albidum), which is native to Eastern North America. Unlike many herbs and spices that come from various parts of the world, filé powder has a unique regional significance and is not commonly used in a wide range of international cuisines. It is a traditional ingredient, deeply rooted in the culinary traditions of Louisiana.

Culinary Uses

Filé powder is best known as a thickening and flavoring agent in gumbo, where it adds a distinctive earthy note and contributes to the dish's signature texture. It is typically stirred into the pot at the end of cooking, as simmering it can cause the gumbo to become stringy. Besides gumbo, filé powder can be used to season stews, soups, and other dishes, adding depth and a slight woodsy aroma. It pairs well with the bold flavors of Cajun and Creole seasonings, seafood, poultry, and smoked meats.

Medicinal Properties

Historically, the sassafras tree, from which filé powder is made, was used in various forms of traditional medicine, including as a treatment for a variety of ailments such as skin diseases, rheumatism, and fever. Sassafras root bark was once used to flavor root beer until it was banned by the FDA in 1960 due to health concerns associated with safrole, a compound found in the plant. However, filé powder, made from the leaves, contains only trace amounts of safrole.

Cultural Significance

Filé powder holds a special place in the culinary history of the Southern United States, especially Louisiana, where it is a key ingredient in Creole and Cajun cooking. Its use is a testament to the Native American heritage of the region, as it was originally introduced to European settlers by the Choctaw Indians. It embodies the rich blend of cultural influences that characterize Louisiana cuisine, including Native American, African, French, and Spanish.

Production

The production of filé powder is relatively simple but labor-intensive, involving the harvesting, drying, and grinding of sassafras leaves. While it is not produced on a large industrial scale like many common spices, it is available from specialty spice vendors and in stores that cater to Southern or specifically Louisiana cooking.

Fingerroot

Fingerroot, known for its distinctive shape and aromatic qualities, is a valued herb and spice in Southeast Asian cuisine. Fingerroot (Boesenbergia rotunda), also known as Chinese ginger, krachai, or Thai ginger, belongs to the ginger family, Zingiberaceae. It is native to China, India, and Southeast Asia. This perennial herb is characterized by its long, finger-like rhizomes, which are pale yellow on the inside and have a skin that ranges from light brown to pinkish.

Culinary Uses

Fingerroot's flavor is slightly spicy and peppery, with a hint of ginger and citrus. It is an essential ingredient in Thai, Indonesian, and Malaysian cuisines, used in curries, soups, salads, and seafood dishes. The rhizomes can be used fresh, dried, or pickled, and are often ground into a paste as a base for various spice blends. Fingerroot pairs well with lemongrass, galangal, turmeric, and coconut milk, enhancing the complexity of flavors in traditional dishes like Thai green curry, rendang, and tom yum soup. It is valued not just for its flavor but also for its ability to tenderize meat and seafood.

Medicinal Properties

Fingerroot is believed to aid in digestion, relieve stomach discomfort, and treat skin infections. Recent studies have also investigated its potential benefits in reducing blood sugar levels and improving cholesterol profiles, although more research is needed to fully understand its health impacts.

Cultural Significance

In Southeast Asia, fingerroot is more than just a culinary ingredient; it is part of the region's rich herbal medicine tradition. Its use in traditional recipes and remedies reflects the deep cultural knowledge and appreciation of natural ingredients for both their flavor and health benefits.

Production

Fingerroot is mainly cultivated in tropical regions of Southeast Asia, including Thailand, Indonesia, and Malaysia. The herb thrives in moist, shaded areas and is harvested for its rhizomes. While not as widely known or available internationally as other members of the ginger family, fingerroot is increasingly being recognized and sought after for its unique flavor and potential health benefits.

Galangal, greater

Galangal, specifically greater galangal (Alpinia galanga), is a robust and aromatic rhizome that plays a crucial role in Southeast Asian cuisine, akin to its cousin, ginger. It belongs to the ginger family, Zingiberaceae, and is native to Indonesia, and widely used across Southeast Asia, India, and China. This perennial plant is characterized by its long, thin, and tough rhizomes, which have a pale yellow to white interior and a distinct, sharp, and slightly citrusy flavor.

Culinary Uses

Greater galangal's flavor is pungent and sharp, with notes of pine and citrus, distinguishing it from the milder and sweeter taste of lesser galangal. It is a fundamental ingredient in Thai, Indonesian, and Malaysian cooking, used in pastes, curries, soups, and stews. Galangal cannot be substituted with ginger, as its flavor is quite unique, though they share some similarities. It is often used in combination with lemongrass, garlic, turmeric, and chili peppers, contributing to the complex flavor profiles of dishes like Thai tom yum soup, Indonesian rendang, and various curry pastes. The rhizome is usually sliced, grated, or pounded and added to dishes whole or as part of a spice paste.

Medicinal Properties

Traditionally, galangal has been used in herbal medicine to treat various ailments, including digestive issues, inflammation, and infections. It is believed to possess anti-inflammatory, antimicrobial, and antioxidant properties, making it a valuable ingredient in traditional remedies for colds, sore throat, and stomach discomfort.

Cultural Significance

In Southeast Asia, galangal is more than just a culinary herb; it is an integral part of the region's herbal medicine and culinary traditions. Its use reflects the deep interconnection between food and wellness in these cultures, where many ingredients serve both nutritional and medicinal purposes.

Production

Galangal is primarily cultivated in Southeast Asia, with Thailand, Indonesia, and Malaysia being notable producers. The plant requires a tropical climate to thrive and is harvested for its rhizomes, which are the most valued part of the plant. Fresh, dried, and powdered forms of galangal are available, though the fresh rhizome is preferred for its superior flavor and aromatic qualities.

Galangal, lesser

Lesser galangal (Alpinia officinarum), distinct from its relative greater galangal, is a valued spice and medicinal herb in Asian and especially Southeast Asian cuisine. It belongs to the ginger family, Zingiberaceae, and is native to China, spreading to parts of Southeast Asia. This perennial plant features slender stems, long leaves, and small, reddish-white flowers. The rhizomes are smaller, darker, and more aromatic than those of greater galangal, with a spicy, sweet taste that is somewhat reminiscent of cinnamon.

Culinary Uses

Lesser galangal's flavor is sharp and spicy, with hints of pepper and a subtle sweetness, making it a unique ingredient in culinary applications. It is used in a variety of Asian dishes, including soups, curries, and marinades, contributing a complex flavor profile. In Indonesian cuisine, it is an essential spice for making traditional dishes like soto and rendang. The rhizomes can be sliced, grated, or ground into a powder and added to recipes. Lesser galangal pairs well with other spices such as turmeric, lemongrass, and chili peppers, enhancing the flavors of seafood, meats, and vegetables.

Medicinal Properties

Traditionally, lesser galangal has been used in Asian herbal medicine for its digestive, anti-inflammatory, and expectorant properties. It is believed to aid in digestion, relieve abdominal discomfort, and reduce inflammation. The rhizome contains several compounds, including galangin and eugenol, which are thought to contribute to its medicinal effects.

Cultural Significance

In Asian cultures, lesser galangal is not only a culinary ingredient but also a component of traditional medicine. Its use in cooking and healing practices reflects the holistic approach to wellness, where food and medicine are often intertwined.

Production

Lesser galangal is primarily cultivated in Southeast Asia, with China being a significant producer. The plant thrives in tropical climates and is harvested for its aromatic rhizomes. While not as widely available as greater galangal, lesser galangal can be found in Asian markets and specialty stores in fresh, dried, or powdered form.

Garlic

Garlic, renowned for its pungent aroma and strong flavor, is an indispensable ingredient in cuisines around the globe. Garlic (Allium sativum) belongs to the Allium family, which also includes onions, leeks, and chives. It is native to Central Asia and northeastern Iran but has been cultivated worldwide for thousands of years. Garlic is a perennial plant, characterized by its bulb, which is divided into numerous cloves, each enclosed in a thin, papery skin.

Culinary Uses

Garlic's flavor is robust, warm, and slightly spicy, making it a foundational element in a myriad of dishes across various cuisines, including Italian, Chinese, Indian, Middle Eastern, and Mexican. It is used in its raw form, minced, crushed, or roasted, to flavor sauces, soups, stews, marinades, dressings, and meat dishes. Garlic pairs well with a wide range of ingredients, including tomatoes, onions, basil, parsley, and proteins from meats to beans. Its versatility allows it to be a key ingredient in iconic dishes such as garlic bread, aglio e olio pasta, and garlic-infused oils. Garlic is often added at different stages of cooking, depending on the desired intensity of flavor; it provides a more pungent taste when raw and becomes sweeter and milder when cooked.

Medicinal Properties

Garlic contains allicin, a compound that is believed to have anti-inflammatory, antibacterial, and antiviral properties, making it effective in fighting infections and boosting the immune system. It is also rich in antioxidants, which can help protect against oxidative stress and may reduce the risk of chronic diseases.

Cultural Significance

Garlic holds a significant place in many cultures, not only as a culinary staple but also for its purported protective powers against evil spirits and vampires in folklore. In traditional medicine, it has been used to treat a range of conditions, from colds to wounds. Garlic festivals and celebrations worldwide attest to its popularity and importance in culinary traditions.

Production

China is the largest producer of garlic, followed by India, South Korea, Egypt, and Russia. It is grown by planting individual cloves in the ground, which then develop into full bulbs. Garlic is harvested for its bulbs, and both the cloves and the sprouted greens (garlic scapes) are used in cooking.

Garlic chives

Garlic chives, known for their delicate garlic flavor, are a popular herb in Asian cuisines, particularly in Chinese, Japanese, and Korean dishes. Garlic chives (Allium tuberosum) belong to the Amaryllidaceae family, closely related to onions, garlic, and chives. They are native to the Chinese region but have become a staple in many parts of the world. This perennial herb is characterized by its flat, grass-like leaves and beautiful white flowers, making it not only a culinary favorite but also a decorative plant in gardens.

Culinary Uses

The flavor of garlic chives is more subtle than garlic, offering a mild garlic-onion taste. They are used extensively in Asian cuisine, including in dumplings, stir-fries, soups, and as a garnish for noodle dishes and omelets. Garlic chives pair well with eggs, seafood, pork, and a variety of vegetables. They can be used fresh or cooked, adding a layer of flavor to dishes without overpowering them. The flowers and flower buds of garlic chives are also edible and often used in salads and as garnishes for their slight garlicky flavor and aesthetic appeal.

Medicinal Properties

Traditionally, garlic chives have been used in herbal medicine for their digestive, anti-inflammatory, and antiseptic properties. They are rich in vitamins A and C, calcium, and iron.

Cultural Significance

In Asian cultures, garlic chives hold a place not only in the kitchen for their culinary uses but also in traditional medicine for their health benefits. In Japan, garlic chives are called 'nira' and are used in a variety of dishes, symbolizing vitality and health.

Production

Garlic chives are widely cultivated in China, Japan, and Korea, and they have also gained popularity in home gardens around the world, including in the United States and Europe. They are easy to grow, preferring well-drained soil and full sun to partial shade. They are harvested for their leaves, which can be cut several times in a growing season.

Other Facts

Garlic chives are not only valued for their culinary uses but also for their ornamental appeal. The plant's white flowers attract bees and butterflies, contributing to pollination in gardens.

Ginger

Ginger, known for its pungent and spicy flavor, is a fundamental herb and spice in global cuisine, particularly in Asian, Indian, and Caribbean dishes. Ginger (Zingiber officinale) belongs to the Zingiberaceae family, which also includes turmeric and cardamom. It is native to Southeast Asia but has been widely cultivated in other tropical regions around the world. Ginger is a perennial plant, characterized by its thick, fibrous rhizome (root), which is the part most commonly used in cooking and medicine. The rhizome can vary in color from yellow, white, to red, depending on the variety.

Culinary Uses

Ginger's flavor is warm, robust, and slightly sweet, with a fiery, peppery finish that can enhance both savory and sweet dishes. It is a versatile ingredient used fresh, dried, powdered, or as an oil or juice. In cooking, ginger is essential in a myriad of dishes such as stir-fries, soups, curries, marinades, and sweets like gingerbread and ginger cookies. It pairs well with garlic, soy sauce, citrus, and honey, making it a staple in many sauces and glazes. In beverages, ginger is celebrated in teas, smoothies, and traditional drinks like ginger beer and ginger ale.

Medicinal Properties

Ginger has been used for thousands of years for its medicinal properties. It is renowned for its ability to aid digestion, relieve nausea, and reduce inflammation. The root contains gingerol, a bioactive compound with powerful anti-inflammatory and antioxidant effects, which can help alleviate symptoms of gastrointestinal distress, reduce soreness and pain, and boost the immune system. Ginger is also commonly used in remedies for colds and flu due to its warming and soothing properties.

Cultural Significance

Ginger holds a significant place in many cultures, not just as a culinary ingredient but also for its medicinal and spiritual values. In Ayurveda, the traditional Indian system of medicine, ginger is considered a key herb for balancing the body. In Chinese medicine, it is used to help warm the body's interior and expel cold.

Production

India is the largest producer of ginger, followed by other countries like China, Nepal, and Indonesia. The cultivation of ginger requires a warm, humid climate, with well-drained, nutrient-rich soil. The plant is grown from rhizomes, which are planted and harvested by hand after the leaves wither, usually 8 to 10 months after planting.

Golpar

Golpar, also known as Persian hogweed (Heracleum persicum), is a unique and aromatic herb indigenous to Iran and some surrounding regions. Unlike basil and other more universally known herbs, golpar is primarily found in Persian, Afghan, and other Middle Eastern cuisines. It belongs to the Apiaceae family, which also includes carrots, celery, and parsley. This plant is characterized by its large, umbel-shaped flowers and broad, serrated leaves. The seeds of the golpar plant are what is most commonly used in culinary applications, often ground into a fine powder.

Culinary Uses

Golpar's flavor is distinctively bitter with earthy and floral undertones, setting it apart from other culinary herbs. It is used to season beans, lentils, and various vegetable dishes, imparting a unique aroma and taste. Golpar is also sprinkled on traditional Iranian dishes such as ash (a thick soup) and kuku (vegetable and herb frittatas), and is used in the spice blend for pickling vegetables. Its flavor complements the rich, savory profiles of stews and grilled meats as well. Due to its strong flavor, it is used sparingly, and is often mixed with other spices and herbs to balance its intensity.

Medicinal Properties

Traditionally, golpar has been used in Persian herbal medicine for its digestive and carminative properties. It is believed to relieve flatulence, stimulate appetite, and aid in the digestion of heavy foods. The seeds are also used for their antiseptic and antimicrobial properties, making them beneficial in treating various ailments.

Cultural Significance

In Persian culture, golpar is more than just a culinary herb; it is a component of the rich tapestry of Persian herbal knowledge and cuisine. It is often used in traditional Nowruz (Persian New Year) dishes and is valued for its medicinal properties as well as its unique flavor. Golpar's use in Persian cooking reflects the importance of herbs in enhancing the flavor and nutritional value of dishes.

Production

Golpar is primarily harvested in Iran and some parts of the Middle East and Central Asia. The plant grows in mountainous regions, and the seeds are collected, dried, and then ground into a powder for culinary use. While not as widely available as other herbs in global markets, golpar can be found in Middle Eastern grocery stores or specialty spice shops.

Grains of paradise

Grains of Paradise, known for their piquant and slightly peppery flavor, are a prized spice originating from West Africa, particularly from countries like Ghana, Nigeria, and Liberia. Grains of Paradise (Aframomum melegueta) belong to the ginger family, Zingiberaceae, and are often used as an alternative to black pepper in African, Middle Eastern, and European cuisines. This spice is harvested from the plant's fruit, which encases the small, reddish-brown seeds. Despite their name, Grains of Paradise are not grains but seeds that offer a complex flavor profile combining elements of pepper, cardamom, and coriander.

Culinary Uses

Grains of Paradise are celebrated for their unique taste, which is warm, spicy, and with a hint of citrus. They are utilized whole, crushed, or ground into powder to season meats, seafood, and vegetable dishes, enhancing flavors with their vibrant, aromatic warmth. This spice is a key ingredient in North and West African cooking, used in traditional stews, soups, and spice blends, such as the Moroccan ras el hanout. In European cuisine, particularly in Scandinavian countries, Grains of Paradise are used to flavor spirits and beers, adding a spicy, peppery note.

Medicinal Properties

Traditionally, Grains of Paradise have been used in African herbal medicine for their digestive and diuretic properties. They are believed to aid in digestion, relieve stomach pain, and promote intestinal health.

Cultural Significance

Grains of Paradise hold a significant place in African cultural traditions, not only as a culinary spice but also in ceremonial and healing practices. In medieval Europe, they were highly valued as a trading commodity and used as a luxurious substitute for black pepper. The spice's name itself reflects its exotic origins and the high esteem in which it was held by European traders and consumers.

Production

The production of Grains of Paradise is mainly concentrated in West Africa, where the climate and soil conditions are ideal for cultivating the Aframomum melegueta plant. The seeds are typically harvested by hand, dried, and then exported to various parts of the world. Although not as widely available as other spices, Grains of Paradise can be found in specialty spice shops, online, or in markets catering to African and Middle Eastern cuisines.

Grains of Selim

Grains of Selim, also known as African Negro Pepper or Kani pepper (Xylopia aethiopica), is a unique spice native to West Africa, particularly prevalent in the cuisines of countries like Senegal, Ghana, and Nigeria. It belongs to the Annonaceae family, which includes other aromatic and medicinal plants. Grains of Selim are obtained from a tall, evergreen tree and are characterized by their twisted, dark brown to black seed pods. Each pod encases multiple seeds that offer a complex flavor profile.

Culinary Uses

The flavor of Grains of Selim is pungent and peppery with a slightly bitter, musky, and smoky undertone. They are used whole or ground into powder and added to soups, stews, and other savory dishes. The spice is an integral part of traditional West African cuisine, often used in spice blends, dry rubs for meats, and as a seasoning for rice dishes and sauces. Grains of Selim are also used to flavor beverages, including teas and local brews, imparting a distinctive warm and spicy note.

Medicinal Properties

Traditionally, Grains of Selim have been used in African herbal medicine for their antiseptic, anti-inflammatory, and analgesic properties. They are believed to aid digestion, relieve stomach pain, and treat respiratory conditions like asthma and bronchitis. The pods are also used as a natural remedy for enhancing fertility and treating a range of other health issues.

Cultural Significance

In West African cultures, Grains of Selim are not only valued for their culinary uses but also for their medicinal and spiritual significance. They are often used in traditional rituals and ceremonies and are believed to possess protective qualities. The spice is a symbol of the rich culinary heritage of the region and is deeply intertwined with the traditional practices and lifestyles of the people.

Production

Grains of Selim are mainly harvested in the wild forests of West Africa. The seed pods are collected, dried, and either sold whole or ground into powder. While not widely known or available internationally, the spice can be found in African grocery stores or specialty spice shops catering to African cuisine.

Hoja santa

Hoja santa, known for its aromatic leaves, is a distinctive herb used in Mexican and Central American cuisines. Hoja santa (Piper auritum) belongs to the Piperaceae family, which also includes black pepper and kava. It is native to the tropical regions of Southern Mexico, Guatemala, and Northern South America. This perennial herb is characterized by its large, heart-shaped leaves, which can grow up to a foot or more in length. The name "hoja santa" translates to "sacred leaf" in Spanish, reflecting its esteemed status in regional culinary and medicinal traditions.

Culinary Uses

Hoja santa's flavor is complex, with notes of anise, eucalyptus, licorice, and black pepper. It is used both fresh and dried to season a variety of dishes, including moles, tamales, soups, and stews. The leaves are sometimes wrapped around fish, chicken, or cheese, imparting a unique flavor during cooking. In addition to its use as a seasoning, hoja santa is also employed as an aromatic wrapper for meats and cheeses, and its large leaves can serve as a natural foil for grilling or steaming.

Medicinal Properties

Traditionally, hoja santa has been used in herbal medicine for its purported digestive and anti-inflammatory properties. It is believed to aid in the treatment of various ailments, such as stomachaches, respiratory conditions, and rheumatism. The leaves contain compounds with antimicrobial and analgesic effects, making them beneficial in soothing skin irritations and minor wounds.

Cultural Significance

In Mexico and Central America, hoja santa is deeply ingrained in the cultural fabric, utilized not only in cooking but also in traditional medicine and religious rituals. The herb is associated with protection and is often planted near homes to ward off evil spirits, echoing the cultural significance of basil in other traditions.

Production

Hoja santa is cultivated in tropical and subtropical climates, primarily in its native regions of Mexico and Central America. The plant thrives in humid, shaded areas and is often grown in home gardens and small-scale farms. It is harvested for its leaves, which are used fresh to maximize their aromatic properties.

Horseradish

Horseradish, known for its pungent and spicy flavor, is a perennial plant used as a condiment or spice in various cuisines around the world. Horseradish (Armoracia rusticana) belongs to the Brassicaceae family, which also includes mustard, wasabi, broccoli, and cabbage. It is native to Southeastern Europe and Western Asia but has become widely cultivated in other parts of the world, including the United States and Canada. The plant is characterized by its large, white, tapering root and broad, crinkled leaves.

Culinary Uses

Horseradish's flavor is intensely sharp, peppery, and sinus-clearing, most commonly used in its grated form as a condiment for meats, sandwiches, and salads. It is a key ingredient in cocktail sauces, often paired with ketchup or tomato sauce, and served with seafood, especially shrimp. Horseradish sauce, made by mixing the grated root with vinegar and sometimes cream or mayonnaise, is a traditional accompaniment to roast beef in British cuisine. Its potent flavor pairs well with rich and fatty foods, cutting through the heaviness with its spicy kick.

Medicinal Properties

Traditionally, horseradish has been used for its medicinal properties, including as a diuretic, to relieve respiratory conditions, and to combat infections due to its antibacterial properties. The root contains high levels of vitamin C, glucosinolates, and other compounds that are believed to stimulate digestion, support immune function, and act as antioxidants.

Cultural Significance

Horseradish has a long history of use, both culinarily and medicinally, dating back to ancient times. In Jewish tradition, it is one of the bitter herbs consumed during the Passover Seder, symbolizing the bitter hardship of slavery in Egypt. Its cultivation and use in Europe and America have historical roots, with the plant being valued for its flavor and health benefits.

Production

Horseradish is primarily cultivated for its large, white roots, which are harvested in the fall. The United States, particularly Illinois, is one of the leading producers of horseradish, along with parts of Europe and Asia. The plant prefers well-drained, fertile soil and full sun to partial shade. After harvesting, the roots can be stored for several months under proper conditions before being processed.

Huacatay

Huacatay, known for its distinctive aroma and flavor, is a vital herb in South American cuisine, particularly in Peru and Bolivia. Huacatay (Tagetes minuta) belongs to the Asteraceae family, which also includes marigolds, daisies, and sunflowers. It is native to the Andean region of South America. This annual herb is characterized by its small, green leaves and yellow flowers. Huacatay is often referred to as Peruvian black mint, although it does not belong to the mint family.

Culinary Uses

Huacatay's flavor is unique, with a complex profile that includes hints of mint, basil, lime, and tarragon. It is used both fresh and dried to season meats, soups, and stews. One of its most famous culinary applications is in the preparation of a green sauce known as "salsa de huacatay," which accompanies traditional Peruvian dishes such as grilled meats, potatoes, and corn. The herb is also used to flavor the traditional Andean beverage chicha and is an ingredient in the marinade for anticuchos, a popular Peruvian street food made from grilled skewered meat.

Medicinal Properties

Traditionally, huacatay has been used in South American herbal medicine for its antiseptic, antifungal, and digestive properties. It is believed to aid in the treatment of digestive issues, respiratory conditions, and to relieve muscle pain. The herb is also used in natural remedies to repel insects and treat insect bites due to its strong aroma.

Cultural Significance

In the Andean region, huacatay holds a special place in culinary traditions, reflecting the rich biodiversity of the area and its importance in indigenous cultures. The herb is used in traditional festivals and religious ceremonies, symbolizing purity and protection.

Production

Huacatay is cultivated in various parts of South America, thriving in temperate to subtropical climates. The plant is grown for its leaves, which are harvested before the plant flowers for optimal flavor. While not as widely known internationally as other herbs, huacatay is available in Latin American markets and specialty stores outside of South America, often in dried or paste form.

Hyssop

Hyssop, celebrated for its aromatic and medicinal qualities, is a herbaceous plant belonging to the mint family, Lamiaceae. Scientifically known as Hyssopus officinalis, hyssop is native to Southern Europe, the Middle East, and the region surrounding the Caspian Sea. It is a perennial herb, recognized by its slender, woody stems, narrow leaves, and spikes of small, blue, pink, or, less commonly, white flowers. Hyssop has been cultivated for centuries, both as a medicinal herb and for its uses in religious and cleansing rituals.

Culinary Uses

Hyssop's flavor is intense and slightly bitter, with hints of mint and camphor. It is used sparingly in cooking due to its strong taste. In culinary applications, hyssop leaves can be added to salads, soups, and stews or used as a garnish. The herb pairs well with rich, fatty foods, helping to cut through the heaviness of dishes. It is also infused in liqueurs and spirits, imparting a unique aromatic quality. Due to its potent flavor, hyssop is often used dried rather than fresh, allowing for a more subtle integration into dishes.

Medicinal Properties

Traditionally, hyssop has been valued for its medicinal properties, including its ability to aid digestion, relieve respiratory conditions, and act as an antiseptic. It is believed to have expectorant properties, making it beneficial in treating coughs and congestion. Hyssop oil, extracted from the leaves and flowers, is used in aromatherapy for its purported ability to relieve anxiety and fatigue.

Cultural Significance

Hyssop holds a special place in various cultural and religious contexts. It is mentioned in the Bible for its purifying and cleansing attributes, symbolizing spiritual cleanliness and redemption. In traditional practices, hyssop has been used in protection rituals and to ward off evil spirits.

Production

Hyssop is cultivated in herb gardens worldwide, valued both for its ornamental beauty and its utility as a herb. It thrives in sunny locations.

Other Facts

Hyssop also attracts beneficial insects, such as bees and butterflies, making it an excellent choice for ecological gardening. The plant's essential oil is used in the production of perfumes and soaps, thanks to its distinctive, refreshing scent.

Jasmine

Jasmine, renowned for its intensely fragrant flowers, is a key component in both culinary and aromatic traditions worldwide. Belonging to the olive family, Oleaceae, jasmine encompasses several species, with the most common being Jasminum officinale and Jasminum sambac. Native to warm temperate and tropical regions of Eurasia, Africa, and Oceania, jasmine plants are perennial, showcasing lush, green leaves and delicate white or yellow flowers. Jasmine has been cultivated for centuries, not only for its beauty and fragrance but also for its use in teas, perfumes, and traditional medicine.

Culinary Uses

Jasmine's flowers are celebrated for their sweet, highly aromatic fragrance. While the flowers themselves are not typically eaten, they are widely used to flavor teas, particularly green tea, creating the famous jasmine tea known for its relaxing properties and delicate taste. In some cultures, jasmine flowers are used in cooking to impart flavor to desserts, such as puddings and jams, or to scent rice dishes. The essence of jasmine is also used in flavoring syrups and liqueurs, offering a subtle, sweet floral note.

Medicinal Properties

Traditionally, jasmine has been used for its potential health benefits, including its soothing effect on the nervous system, which can aid in reducing anxiety and promoting restful sleep. Its antioxidant properties are believed to help strengthen the immune system. Jasmine tea, in particular, is consumed for its calming effects and as a digestive aid. The essential oil derived from jasmine flowers is used in aromatherapy to relieve stress, improve mood, and increase alertness.

Cultural Significance

Jasmine holds a place of honor in many cultures around the world. In Thailand, it symbolizes motherhood and love and is used in offerings and garlands. In Indonesia, jasmine is the national flower, symbolizing purity, eternal life, and nobility. Its pervasive fragrance and beautiful blooms have made it a symbol of beauty and sensuality in various literary and religious contexts.

Production

Major producers of jasmine include India, Egypt, and China, where it is cultivated primarily for its flowers, used in the production of tea, perfumes, and essential oils. Growing jasmine requires a warm climate, well-drained soil, and plenty of sunlight.

Jakhya

Jakhya, a lesser-known but intriguing herb, is a traditional spice native to the Indian subcontinent, particularly in the hill regions of Uttarakhand. Unlike the widely recognized basil, Jakhya (Cleome viscosa) belongs to the Cleomaceae family and is characterized by its tiny, dark seeds that are used as a spice in local cuisines. This annual herb is distinguished by its sticky leaves and stems, with small, yellow flowers that bloom into round, pod-like fruits containing the seeds.

Culinary Uses

Jakhya seeds are primarily used as a seasoning in traditional Uttarakhandi dishes, offering a unique and crunchy texture. Their flavor is described as nutty and slightly bitter, making them a distinctive spice in the culinary repertoire of the region. Jakhya seeds are most commonly used for tempering dishes, such as dals (lentil soups), vegetable stir-fries, and chutneys, where they are heated in hot oil to release their aroma and flavor, similar to mustard seeds in other Indian cuisines.

Medicinal Properties

In traditional medicine, Jakhya seeds have been utilized for their health benefits, though scientific research on their medicinal properties is limited compared to more widely known herbs and spices. They are believed to possess digestive and anti-inflammatory properties, aiding in the improvement of digestion and the relief of stomach issues. The plant's leaves and seeds are also used in folk remedies for treating skin conditions and as a natural insect repellent.

Cultural Significance

Jakhya holds a cultural significance in Uttarakhand, where it is not just a culinary ingredient but a part of the traditional agricultural practices and food heritage. It represents the connection of the local population with their environment and traditional farming methods, showcasing the biodiversity of the region and its adaptation to the local climate and soil conditions.

Production

The cultivation of Jakhya is confined to small-scale, traditional farming practices within the Himalayan regions of Uttarakhand. It is not widely commercialized or known outside these areas, making it a unique and regional specialty. Farmers collect the seeds after the plant matures and dries, preserving them for culinary use throughout the year.

Jalapeño

Jalapeño peppers, known for their moderate heat and deep, green flavor, are a staple ingredient in Mexican cuisine and have gained popularity worldwide. Jalapeños (Capsicum annuum) belong to the nightshade family, Solanaceae, and are native to Mexico. They are a type of chili pepper that ranges from green to red as they mature, with the green variety being most commonly used in culinary applications. Jalapeños are perennial plants in their native climate but are often grown as annuals in temperate regions. They are characterized by their smooth, firm, and shiny skin and can vary in heat based on growing conditions and variety.

Culinary Uses

Jalapeño's flavor is bright and piquant, with a heat level that is approachable for many palates, making it versatile in culinary use. It is a key ingredient in Mexican dishes such as salsas, tacos, and nachos. Jalapeños are also popular for stuffing, as in jalapeño poppers, where they are filled with cheese and sometimes breaded and fried. They can be diced into stews and soups, sliced for garnishes, or pickled for a tangy, spicy condiment. Jalapeños pair well with a wide range of ingredients, including meats, cheeses, and vegetables, adding a spicy kick to dishes without overwhelming other flavors. They are also used to flavor sauces and oils.

Medicinal Properties

Traditionally, jalapeños have been used for their health benefits, including their ability to boost metabolism and aid in weight loss due to the presence of capsaicin, which is responsible for their heat. Jalapeños are rich in vitamins A and C and potassium, contributing to overall health by supporting the immune system, maintaining healthy skin, and reducing the risk of chronic diseases.

Cultural Significance

Jalapeños hold a significant place in Mexican culture, symbolizing the vibrant and spicy flavors characteristic of the country's cuisine.

Production

Mexico remains the leading producer of jalapeños, but they are also widely cultivated in the United States, particularly in Texas and New Mexico, where they are a key ingredient in Tex-Mex cuisine. Jalapeños are grown both in open fields and under cover in regions with suitable climates. They are harvested at different stages of maturity for various culinary uses, from the younger, milder green peppers to the fully ripe, hotter red peppers.

Jimbu

Jimbu, an aromatic herb, is an integral part of Nepalese cuisine, where it is cherished for both its culinary and medicinal properties. Jimbu (Allium hypsistum) belongs to the onion family, Alliaceae, and is found predominantly in the Himalayan regions of Nepal, as well as parts of India and Bhutan. It is a perennial plant, characterized by its slender, grass-like leaves and small, bulbous roots. The dried leaves and flowers of jimbu are what are primarily used in cooking, imparting a distinct flavor that is somewhat a cross between onion and chives, with a unique, slightly earthy aroma.

Culinary Uses

Jimbu's flavor is subtle yet distinctive, with a mild onion-like taste that is less pungent than garlic or onion, making it a beloved ingredient in traditional Nepalese dishes. It is most commonly used in tempered dishes, where it is fried in fat or oil at the beginning of cooking to release its aroma and flavor. This technique is essential in preparing dal (lentil soup), curries, and pickles, providing a depth of flavor that is characteristic of Himalayan cuisine. Jimbu is also used in the preparation of meat dishes, adding a layer of flavor that complements the natural tastes of the ingredients.

Medicinal Properties

Traditionally, jimbu has been valued for its medicinal properties, including its ability to aid digestion and alleviate stomach ailments. It is believed to have antifungal and antibacterial properties, making it useful in treating infections and preserving food. In local practices, jimbu is also used to treat common colds and sore throats, either by consuming it in food or using it in herbal remedies.

Cultural Significance

Jimbu holds a special place in Nepalese culture, being an essential component of their culinary heritage. Its use is deeply ingrained in the cooking traditions of the Himalayan people, symbolizing the blending of flavors and traditions in Nepalese cuisine. The harvesting of jimbu, which involves collecting the wild herb from high-altitude regions, is a practice that connects the people with their environment and traditions.

Production

Jimbu is primarily wild-harvested in the mountainous regions of Nepal, making it a unique and somewhat rare commodity. Its cultivation is limited, due to the specific altitudinal and climatic conditions it requires to thrive. The dried herb is often found in local markets throughout Nepal and in stores specializing in South Asian ingredients internationally.

Juniper berry

Juniper berry, distinct for its piney flavor and aromatic qualities, plays a pivotal role in culinary and medicinal traditions across various cultures. Juniper berries are not true berries but the female seed cone produced by the various species of junipers (Juniperus spp.), which belong to the cypress family, Cupressaceae. They are native to cool temperate regions of the Northern Hemisphere, from North America to Europe and Asia. The small, blue-black berries are actually modified cones with unusually fleshy and merged scales, giving them a berry-like appearance. Juniper is an evergreen shrub or tree, characterized by its needle-like leaves and the distinct, sharp flavor of its berries.

Culinary Uses

Juniper berries are best known for their role in flavoring gin, a testament to their potent, aromatic qualities. However, their culinary use extends beyond spirits; they are a traditional ingredient in European cuisine, particularly in dishes from Scandinavian, Eastern European, and Western European countries. The berries impart a sharp, clear flavor with piney and slightly citrusy notes, making them ideal for gamey meats like venison, duck, and wild boar. They are also used to season pork, sauerkraut, and cabbage dishes, as well as in marinades and as a spice in pickling processes.

Medicinal Properties

Essential oil extracted from juniper berries is used in aromatherapy to relieve stress and anxiety, and their antioxidant components contribute to their health benefits, including anti-inflammatory effects.

Cultural Significance

In European folklore, juniper is believed to ward off evil spirits. Its use in gin production also carries historical significance, dating back to the 17th century in the Netherlands, where it was initially consumed for medicinal purposes before evolving into the popular spirit known today.

Production

Juniper berries are harvested from wild populations as well as from cultivated plants. While not as widely cultivated on a commercial scale as other herbs and spices, juniper plays a niche yet significant role in the culinary and beverage industries.

Other Facts

Juniper berries mature over two to three years, changing color from green to a dark blue-black hue when ripe. Only the ripe berries are harvested for use in cooking and distillation.

Kaffir lime

Kaffir lime, known for its distinctively fragrant leaves and fruit, plays an essential role in Southeast Asian cuisine. The Kaffir lime (Citrus hystrix), also referred to in more culturally sensitive terms as "makrut lime," belongs to the citrus family, Rutaceae, and is native to tropical Asia, including parts of India, Thailand, Indonesia, and the Philippines. It is a perennial tree, characterized by its bumpy, green fruit and glossy, dark green leaves that are double-lobed, resembling a figure-8.

Culinary Uses

The leaves of the Kaffir lime are highly valued for their aromatic, floral, and citrus notes, which are released when bruised or cooked. They are a key ingredient in Thai cuisine, used in curries, soups like Tom Yum, and salads for their distinct lemon-lime flavor that cannot be easily substituted. The zest of the Kaffir lime fruit is also used to add a piquant flavor to dishes and pastes, while the juice, though less commonly used due to its bitterness, can be found in some recipes to add acidity. The leaves are often used whole in cooking and removed before serving or finely chopped to be incorporated into dishes.

Medicinal Properties

Traditionally, Kaffir lime has been used in herbal medicine for its digestive, oral health, and detoxifying properties. The oil from the leaves and rind is thought to have antiseptic and anti-inflammatory qualities, making it beneficial for skin care and treating various ailments. The fruit's juice and rind are used in traditional remedies for digestion and as a natural cleanser.

Cultural Significance

In Southeast Asia, the Kaffir lime holds significant cultural value, not just in cuisine but also in health and spirituality. It is used in rituals for cleansing and purifying and is believed to ward off evil spirits. The tree itself is often planted around homes for its protective properties and to provide a ready supply of its aromatic leaves and fruit.

Production

The Kaffir lime tree is cultivated in tropical and subtropical regions worldwide, with Thailand being a prominent producer due to the high demand for its leaves and zest in Thai cuisine. The tree thrives in humid climates with well-drained soil and can be grown in home gardens where conditions allow or in pots in cooler climates, although indoor plants may not produce fruit as prolifically..

Kala zeera

Kala zeera, also known as black cumin or Bunium persicum, is a highly valued spice, particularly in South Asian and Middle Eastern cuisines. Unlike the more common cumin (Cuminum cyminum), kala zeera belongs to the Apiaceae family and is native to high-altitude regions of Northern India, Pakistan, Afghanistan, and surrounding areas. It is a biennial herb, characterized by its fine, feathery leaves, small white flowers, and dark, slender seeds that are the source of its culinary and medicinal use. Kala zeera is prized for its distinctive, earthy flavor, which is richer and less harsh than that of common cumin, with notes of sweetness and a slightly bitter aftertaste.

Culinary Uses

Kala zeera's rich, nutty flavor and aroma make it a cherished spice in the culinary traditions where it is used. It is often added to dishes like curries, stews, and rice dishes to impart its unique taste. In Indian cuisine, it is a component of the spice blend panch phoron, used in Bengali dishes. Kala zeera is also used in the preparation of masalas and as a seasoning for meats and vegetables. Its potent flavor means it is used sparingly and often added at the beginning of cooking to allow its full aroma to infuse the dish.

Medicinal Properties

Traditionally, kala zeera has been used for its health benefits, including digestive aid, anti-inflammatory properties, and as a remedy for respiratory conditions. It is believed to stimulate appetite and aid in digestion, making it a common addition to foods as a natural digestive. The seeds are also used in traditional medicine to treat ailments such as colds, fevers, and asthma due to their expectorant properties.

Cultural Significance

Kala zeera holds a special place in the culinary and medicinal traditions of the regions it originates from. Its use in traditional dishes and home remedies spans centuries, reflecting the spice's integration into cultural practices and its valued role in local cuisines.

Production

The cultivation of kala zeera is primarily confined to the mountainous regions where it is native. The harsh, dry climates and high altitudes of these areas provide the ideal conditions for the plant to develop its distinctive flavor. The seeds are harvested by hand, dried, and then sold whole or ground into a powder. Its limited geographic range and labor-intensive harvest contribute to kala zeera's status as a specialty spice.

Keluak

Keluak, also known as the kepayang or buah keluak, is a distinctive ingredient primarily found in the cuisines of Southeast Asia, especially in Indonesian and Peranakan dishes. The keluak nut comes from the Pangium edule tree, which is native to the mangrove swamps of Southeast Asia, including Indonesia, Malaysia, and Singapore. This tree is part of the Achariaceae family. The fruit of the Pangium edule tree contains seeds that are initially toxic due to cyanogenic glycosides and must undergo a fermentation process to make them edible.

Culinary Uses

Keluak has a unique, earthy flavor often described as similar to truffles, which adds depth to dishes. It is a key ingredient in traditional recipes like Ayam Buah Keluak, a well-known Peranakan (Nyonya) chicken stew, where the nuts are mixed with spices and stuffed back into their shells before being cooked. The nuts can also be ground into a paste and used as a flavoring for gravies and curries, imparting a dark, rich color and intense, smoky flavor. Keluak pairs well with meaty and savory flavors, such as chicken, pork, and beef, enhancing the complexity of the dishes it is added to.

Medicinal Properties

Traditionally, keluak has been used in folk medicine by indigenous communities. The detoxification process it undergoes not only makes the nuts safe for consumption but may also influence their medicinal properties. However, specific health benefits of keluak have not been as extensively documented as those of more commonly known herbs and spices.

Cultural Significance

Its use in Peranakan cuisine, for instance, showcases the blend of Chinese and Malay culinary traditions, symbolizing cultural integration and heritage.

Production

The Pangium edule tree is not widely cultivated on an industrial scale, and keluak nuts are mostly harvested from wild trees. The process of making keluak nuts safe for consumption involves burying them in ash, soil, or a combination of both, and allowing them to ferment for several weeks to several months. This process reduces the cyanide content to safe levels. Due to their initial toxicity, handling and preparing keluak nuts require knowledge and care. The fermentation process not only detoxifies the nuts but also develops their characteristic flavor. Despite their culinary value, the nuts must be treated with respect to ensure they are safe for consumption.

Kencur

Kencur, known for its aromatic rhizome, is a significant herb in many Southeast Asian cuisines, particularly in Indonesia, Thailand, and Malaysia. Kencur (Kaempferia galanga), also referred to as aromatic ginger or sand ginger, belongs to the ginger family, Zingiberaceae. It is native to Southeast Asia and is a perennial plant characterized by its striking, spear-shaped leaves and small, rhizome root system. Unlike its more widely recognized relatives ginger and turmeric, kencur has a milder, somewhat sweet and peppery flavor profile.

Culinary Uses

Kencur's flavor is subtly earthy with a hint of peppery spice, making it a unique ingredient in the culinary world. It is commonly used in traditional Southeast Asian dishes, including Javanese and Balinese cuisines. Kencur is a key ingredient in spice pastes or mixes, such as bumbu, used to flavor meats, seafood, and vegetarian dishes. It is also used in making traditional herbal drinks known as "jamu" in Indonesia, which are believed to have health benefits. The herb pairs well with coconut milk, lemongrass, and other aromatic spices like coriander and cumin. Its delicate flavor is best preserved when added towards the end of the cooking process or used in raw preparations.

Medicinal Properties

The rhizome contains compounds such as cineole and ethyl p-methoxycinnamate, which contribute to its therapeutic effects.

Cultural Significance

Kencur holds a special place in the cultural and culinary traditions of Southeast Asia. It is not only cherished for its unique flavor but also for its role in traditional medicine. In Indonesia, for example, kencur is a staple ingredient in jamu, illustrating the herb's integration into daily health practices and rituals.

Production

Kencur is cultivated primarily in Southeast Asia, where it thrives in the tropical climate. It is grown both in small home gardens and on a larger scale for commercial use.

Other Facts

Kencur is notable for its low profile growth and the beauty of its leaves, making it an attractive addition to tropical gardens..

Kinh gioi

Kinh Gioi, also known as Vietnamese balm or lemon balm, is a cherished herb in Vietnamese cuisine and beyond. Its scientific name is Elsholtzia ciliata, and it belongs to the mint family, Lamiaceae. This herb is native to Asia, thriving in the temperate to subtropical regions of Vietnam, China, Japan, and Korea. Kinh Gioi is characterized by its slender, serrated leaves and a distinctive lemony scent, making it easily distinguishable from other herbs.

Culinary Uses

The flavor of Kinh Gioi is distinctly lemony and minty, with a subtle hint of spice, making it a versatile herb in culinary applications. It is predominantly used in Vietnamese cuisine, where it is added to salads, soups, spring rolls, and fish dishes, imparting a fresh, citrusy aroma and flavor. Kinh Gioi is also brewed as a refreshing tea, either on its own or blended with other herbs. Its vibrant flavor complements chicken, seafood, and vegetable dishes beautifully, and it is often used fresh to garnish or incorporate into salads for a burst of freshness.

Medicinal Properties

Traditionally, Kinh Gioi has been valued for its medicinal properties, particularly in Vietnamese and Chinese herbal medicine. It is believed to have antiseptic, digestive, and calming effects, making it a remedy for various ailments including indigestion, headaches, and even anxiety. The essential oils in Kinh Gioi, particularly citronellal, contribute to its therapeutic benefits.

Cultural Significance

In Vietnam and other parts of Asia, Kinh Gioi holds cultural significance beyond its culinary and medicinal uses. It is often grown in home gardens and used in traditional ceremonies and remedies, reflecting the deep connection between food, health, and cultural practices.

Production

Kinh Gioi is cultivated in Vietnam and other parts of Southeast Asia, usually in small-scale gardens or as part of diversified agricultural systems. It grows well in temperate climates, requiring minimal care beyond regular watering and some sun exposure. While not as widely commercialized as other herbs, Kinh Gioi is a staple in local markets and is becoming increasingly available in international markets, especially in areas with large Vietnamese communities.

Kokum

Kokum, derived from the fruit of the Garcinia indica tree, is a prized culinary and medicinal ingredient indigenous to the Western Ghats of India. This tropical fruit tree belongs to the Clusiaceae family and is revered for its deep purple to blackish, plum-like fruits. The outer cover of the fruit, when dried, is known as kokum, and it is utilized for its sour flavor and health benefits, while the seed is valued for its fat content, known as kokum butter. Kokam also finds applications in cosmetics and traditional Ayurvedic medicine. Kokam butter is prized for its emollient properties, making it a popular ingredient in lotions, creams, and lip balms.

Culinary Uses

Kokum's flavor is predominantly sour with a slight sweetness, making it a unique and versatile ingredient in Indian cuisine. It is extensively used in the coastal regions of Maharashtra, Goa, and Karnataka. Kokum serves as a souring agent in curries, dals, and beverages, much like tamarind but with its distinctive flavor. It is particularly famous for its use in seafood dishes, lentil soups, and refreshing summer drinks like kokum sherbet, which is appreciated for its cooling properties. The dried rind imparts a vibrant red color and a tangy taste to dishes, enhancing their flavor profile.

Medicinal Properties

Kokum has been traditionally utilized for its various health benefits. It is known for its digestive properties, acting as an antidote for indigestion and acidity. The fruit contains hydroxycitric acid (HCA), which is researched for its potential in weight management by suppressing appetite and inhibiting fat production. Additionally, kokum is rich in antioxidants, which help in combating oxidative stress and promoting overall health.

Cultural Significance

Kokum holds a special place in the culinary traditions of the Indian Western Ghats, embodying the essence of coastal cuisine. Its use in traditional recipes and summer beverages highlights its integral role in regional food culture and its adaptation to the local climate. Kokum's medicinal properties are also well recognized in Ayurveda, where it is used in various treatments.

Production

India, particularly the Western Ghats region, is the primary producer of kokum. The trees thrive in the humid, tropical climate of this area. The cultivation of Garcinia indica is crucial for the biodiversity of the region and supports the livelihoods of local communities. The fruits are harvested, and the rinds are sun-dried before being used in culinary applications or medicinal preparations.

Korarima

Korarima, also known as Ethiopian cardamom or false cardamom, is a highly valued spice in the cuisines of East Africa, particularly in Ethiopian and Eritrean dishes. Korarima (Aframomum corrorima) belongs to the ginger family, Zingiberaceae, and is native to the highland regions of Ethiopia and surrounding areas. It is a perennial herb that produces large leafy stalks and pods containing numerous seeds. These seeds are what is primarily used as a spice, offering a flavor profile that is both aromatic and complex, with hints of citrus and eucalyptus.

Culinary Uses

Korarima's flavor is warmly aromatic, somewhat less pungent than true cardamom, with notes of camphor and lemon. It is a staple ingredient in the famous Ethiopian spice blend known as "berbere," as well as in "mitmita," another spicy blend used in Ethiopian cuisine. These blends are crucial for seasoning stews (wats), meats, and vegetables, providing a distinctive taste that is integral to the culinary identity of the region. Korarima can also be used in baking and in coffee, where it imparts a unique flavor that complements the rich aroma of the beans.

Medicinal Properties

Traditionally, korarima has been used in Ethiopian and Eritrean traditional medicine for its health benefits, including digestive aid and stimulant properties. While scientific studies on korarima specifically are limited, its use in traditional medicine highlights its esteemed place in local health practices.

Cultural Significance

In Ethiopia and Eritrea, korarima is not just a spice but a part of the cultural heritage, especially in the context of coffee ceremonies, where it is often added to coffee to enhance its flavor. This practice is deeply ingrained in the social fabric of these countries, signifying hospitality and community. The spice is also used in religious ceremonies and traditional festivals, underscoring its importance beyond the culinary realm.

Production

Korarima is primarily cultivated in Ethiopia, Eritrea, and some parts of Sudan and Kenya. The spice grows in the wild and is also cultivated in gardens and small farms. The pods are harvested manually, and the seeds are extracted and dried before being sold whole or ground. Due to its specific regional growth, korarima is not as widely available internationally as other spices, but it has been gaining popularity due to the global interest in Ethiopian cuisine.

Koseret leaves

Koseret leaves, derived from the Lippia adoensis plant, are a cherished herb in Ethiopian and Eritrean cuisines. This perennial shrub is part of the Verbenaceae family and is native to the highlands of East Africa. Koseret is recognized for its small, lance-shaped leaves, which emit a strong, fragrant aroma reminiscent of lemon and oregano when crushed. The plant is not only valued for its culinary applications but also for its medicinal properties.

Culinary Uses

Koseret leaves have a unique flavor profile that is both citrusy and slightly spicy, making them a distinctive ingredient in East African cooking. They are primarily used in the preparation of spiced clarified butter, known as niter kibbeh in Ethiopia and tesmi in Eritrea. This butter is a foundational element in many traditional dishes, imparting a rich, aromatic flavor to stews, vegetables, and meats. The leaves are also used to season soups and lentil dishes, adding depth and complexity to the cuisine's flavor palette.

Medicinal Properties

Traditionally, koseret leaves have been utilized for their health benefits in East African herbal medicine. They are believed to possess anti-inflammatory and antimicrobial properties, making them useful in treating colds, respiratory issues, and digestive problems. The leaves are sometimes made into a tea, which is consumed for its soothing effects and potential to boost the immune system.

Cultural Significance

In Ethiopia and Eritrea, koseret leaves hold cultural importance beyond their use in everyday cooking. The preparation of niter kibbeh and tesmi using koseret is a time-honored tradition, passed down through generations. These culinary practices are integral to the cultural identity and heritage of the region, celebrating the rich diversity of flavors and ingredients unique to East African cuisine.

Production

Koseret is cultivated in Ethiopia, Eritrea, and neighboring regions, thriving in the highland areas where the climate is conducive to its growth. The herb is harvested for its leaves, which are used both fresh and dried. While koseret is a staple in its native regions, it is less commonly found in international markets, making it a sought-after ingredient among diaspora communities and culinary enthusiasts looking to explore authentic East African flavors.

Kudum Puli

Kudampuli, also known as Malabar tamarind or Garcinia cambogia, is a tropical fruit renowned for its culinary and medicinal properties, particularly in the Indian state of Kerala and other parts of Southeast Asia. This fruit belongs to the Clusiaceae family and grows on the Garcinia gummi-gutta tree. It is characterized by its pumpkin-like shape but is much smaller in size. When ripe, the fruit skin turns a deep reddish-purple. For culinary use, the rinds are sun-dried and then smoked, resulting in a dark, shriveled appearance with a sour and slightly fruity flavor.

Culinary Uses

Kudampuli's flavor is distinctly sour, with a subtle fruity undertone, making it a unique ingredient in the culinary world. It is extensively used in Kerala and Sri Lankan cuisines, particularly in fish curries and seafood dishes, where it imparts a tangy taste that is signature to these regional dishes. Unlike other souring agents like tamarind, kudampuli adds a complex flavor profile to curries and stews, enhancing the overall dish without overpowering it. The dried fruit is soaked in water before being added to dishes, and its extract can also be used to marinate meats.

Medicinal Properties

Kudampuli has been traditionally valued for its potential health benefits, including aiding digestion, promoting weight loss, and acting as an anti-inflammatory agent. The fruit contains hydroxycitric acid (HCA), which has been studied for its effects on appetite suppression and fat metabolism, although results and opinions on its effectiveness vary.

Cultural Significance

The use of kudampuli in fish curries and other traditional dishes represents a culinary tradition passed down through generations, showcasing the unique flavors and ingredients native to this part of the world.

Production

Kudampuli is primarily grown in the Western Ghats of India, particularly in Kerala, as well as in other tropical regions of Asia and Africa where the climate is suitable for the Garcinia gummi-gutta tree. The fruit is harvested, and the rinds are removed, sun-dried, and sometimes smoked, to be used in cooking or medicinal preparations.

Other Facts

Kudampuli is also known in the global market as a dietary supplement for weight loss, due to the popularity of Garcinia cambogia extracts.

Kutjera

Kutjera, also known as desert raisin, bush tomato, or Akudjura, is a native Australian bush food that has been a staple in the diet of Indigenous Australians for thousands of years. The plant (Solanum centrale) belongs to the Solanaceae family, which also includes tomatoes, potatoes, and eggplants. It is a small shrub that produces small fruits, which, when ripe, turn from green to yellow and then to a deep red. These fruits are either consumed fresh or dried, where they resemble raisins in appearance and texture, hence one of its common names, "desert raisin."

Culinary Uses

Kutjera has a strong, distinct flavor that is often described as a mix between a sun-dried tomato, caramel, and tamarind, making it a versatile ingredient in cooking. In its dried form, it is commonly ground into a powder and used as a spice in bread, sauces, chutneys, and meat dishes, particularly with game meats. The rich, tangy flavor of Kutjera adds depth and complexity to dishes, making it a cherished spice in contemporary Australian cuisine, especially in dishes that aim to celebrate and incorporate traditional bush foods.

Medicinal Properties

Traditionally, Indigenous Australians have utilized Kutjera not only as a food source but also for its medicinal properties. While detailed scientific studies on Kutjera's health benefits are limited, it is known to be high in minerals, particularly potassium, and is a good source of vitamins, especially vitamin C. Its consumption is believed to contribute to overall health and well-being, supporting a balanced diet.

Cultural Significance

Kutjera holds significant cultural and spiritual importance among Indigenous Australian communities. It is more than just a food source; it is part of the rich botanical knowledge passed down through generations. The harvesting of Kutjera, like many native bush foods, is intertwined with the traditional land management practices that Indigenous Australians have followed for millennia, showcasing a deep connection with the land and its seasons.

Production

Kutjera is primarily harvested from wild plants growing in the arid regions of Central Australia. Efforts to cultivate it commercially are ongoing, aiming to make this indigenous spice more accessible while ensuring the sustainability of wild populations. The harvesting process is labor-intensive, as it involves collecting the small fruits by hand, then cleaning, drying, and often grinding them into powder.

Lavender

Lavender, celebrated for its fragrant flowers, is a versatile herb used across various domains, from culinary arts to medicinal and aromatic applications. Lavender (Lavandula angustifolia) belongs to the mint family, Lamiaceae, and is native to the Mediterranean region, thriving in sunny, well-drained environments. It is a perennial plant, characterized by its beautiful purple flowers and woody stems. There are several types of lavender, each with its unique scent and flavor profile, including English lavender, French lavender, and Lavandin.

Culinary Uses

Lavender's flavor is floral and slightly sweet, with lemon and citrus notes. It is used in a variety of culinary applications, ranging from desserts and baked goods to savory dishes and beverages. Lavender flowers are often infused into sugar or honey, lending a subtle aroma to cakes, cookies, and teas. The buds can also be used to season meats, like lamb or chicken, and are incorporated into spice rubs and herb blends, such as Herbes de Provence. It is important to use culinary-grade lavender to ensure the flowers are suitable for consumption and to add it sparingly to avoid overpowering dishes.

Medicinal Properties

It is commonly used in aromatherapy to alleviate stress, anxiety, and insomnia. Lavender oil, extracted from the flowers, contains compounds like linalool and linalyl acetate, which are believed to have relaxing effects on the nervous system. The herb is also used to treat minor burns, insect bites, and skin irritations due to its antiseptic and anti-inflammatory qualities.

Cultural Significance

Lavender holds a place of esteem in many cultures for its fragrance and therapeutic benefits. In France, fields of lavender are a hallmark of the Provence region, contributing to the landscape's beauty and economy through the production of lavender oil. The herb is also popular in gardens for its attractiveness to bees and butterflies, as well as its ability to repel pests.

Production

France, Bulgaria, and the United States (notably Washington and California) are among the leading producers of lavender. The plant is cultivated worldwide in temperate climates, both for its aromatic flowers and for the essential oil derived from them. Lavender harvesting occurs in the summer when the flowers are in full bloom and is done by cutting the flower stalks before they fully open.

Lemon balm

Lemon balm, known for its fragrant, lemon-scented leaves, is a cherished herb in culinary, medicinal, and aromatic applications. Lemon balm (Melissa officinalis) belongs to the mint family, Lamiaceae, and is native to South-Central Europe, Iran, and Central Asia, but now grows in temperate regions worldwide. It is a perennial herb, characterized by its bright green leaves, small white or yellowish flowers, and a gentle lemon aroma. Lemon balm is appreciated not only for its pleasant scent and flavor but also for its versatile uses in kitchens and gardens.

Culinary Uses

Lemon balm's flavor is mild and subtly lemony with a hint of mint, making it a versatile herb in both sweet and savory dishes. It is used to flavor teas, desserts, and fruit dishes, adding a fresh, citrusy aroma. Lemon balm can be chopped and added to salads, dressings, and sauces, or used as a garnish for seafood and poultry dishes. Its leaves are also infused in water to make refreshing herbal teas, either on their own or blended with other herbs. The key to using lemon balm in cooking is to add it towards the end of the cooking process to preserve its delicate flavor and aroma.

Medicinal Properties

Traditionally, lemon balm has been used for its calming and digestive properties. It is known to help relieve anxiety, stress, and insomnia due to its mild sedative effects. The herb contains rosmarinic acid, which has antioxidant properties, and essential oils that contribute to its soothing effects. Lemon balm is also used in herbal remedies to treat digestive issues, including indigestion and bloating, and to soothe menstrual cramps and headaches.

Cultural Significance

Lemon balm has been cultivated in the Mediterranean region for over 2,000 years and holds a place in the folklore and herbal medicine traditions of many cultures. In the Middle Ages, it was used to reduce stress and anxiety, promote sleep, and support heart health. The herb was often planted in monastery gardens and used by monks to make medicinal preparations.

Production

While not produced on the scale of major commercial herbs, lemon balm is grown in herb gardens and commercially for its essential oil, particularly in Europe and North America. The plant prefers a sunny location with moist, well-drained soil. Lemon balm is harvested before the flowers fully open to capture the best flavor and aromatic qualities of the leaves.

Lemon ironbark

Lemon Ironbark, known for its distinctive citrus-scented leaves, is a valued herb and spice in Australian cuisine and aromatherapy. Lemon Ironbark (Eucalyptus staigeriana) belongs to the Myrtaceae family and is native to the forests of Queensland and New South Wales, Australia. This tree is characterized by its hard, iron-like bark and lance-shaped leaves that release a strong lemon fragrance when crushed. The essential oil derived from Lemon Ironbark leaves is highly regarded for its aromatic and therapeutic qualities.

Culinary Uses

Lemon Ironbark's flavor is uniquely citrusy with a slight eucalyptal note, making it an intriguing addition to a variety of dishes. It can be used to infuse teas, syrups, and marinades, adding a lemony zest that complements poultry, seafood, and desserts. The leaves, either fresh or dried, can be used sparingly to season dishes directly or included in spice blends to impart a refreshing, lemony essence. Its distinctive flavor profile makes Lemon Ironbark a sought-after ingredient for innovative chefs and home cooks looking to add an Australian twist to their culinary creations.

Medicinal Properties

Traditionally, Lemon Ironbark has been used for its antiseptic and antimicrobial properties, stemming from its rich content of essential oils, particularly citral and eucalyptol. The essential oil is used in aromatherapy to relieve stress, improve concentration, and boost mood. It is also believed to have anti-inflammatory and analgesic properties, making it beneficial for topical application to relieve muscle pain and skin irritations.

Cultural Significance

Lemon Ironbark holds a special place in Indigenous Australian culture, where it has been used for centuries for its medicinal benefits and as a natural insect repellent. The tree's wood and leaves are part of the traditional uses and knowledge of the Australian Aboriginal peoples.

Production

Lemon Ironbark is harvested primarily in its native habitat in Australia. The leaves are collected for their essential oil, which is extracted through steam distillation. This essential oil is highly valued in the perfume industry, as well as in natural health products and culinary applications. Sustainable harvesting practices are important to ensure the longevity and health of wild Lemon Ironbark populations.

Lemon myrtle

Lemon Myrtle, celebrated for its intensely citrus-scented leaves, is a prominent herb in Australian cuisine and aromatherapy. Lemon Myrtle (Backhousia citriodora) is part of the Myrtaceae family and is native to the subtropical rainforests of central and southeastern Queensland, Australia. This evergreen tree is characterized by its glossy green leaves and clusters of white flowers. Lemon Myrtle stands out for having one of the purest concentrations of citral among plants, contributing to its strong lemon scent and flavor, surpassing even that of actual lemons.

Culinary Uses

Lemon Myrtle's flavor is clean and bright, with a deep lemon-lime note that makes it a versatile ingredient in both sweet and savory dishes. It can be used to flavor cakes, cookies, ice cream, and sorbets, as well as being an excellent addition to teas, syrups, and cocktails. In savory dishes, Lemon Myrtle adds a refreshing citrus zest to seafood, chicken, pasta, and risottos. It can be used fresh or dried and ground into a powder, which is the most common form for culinary use. Due to its potent flavor, it is recommended to use Lemon Myrtle sparingly to avoid overwhelming the dish.

Medicinal Properties

It is also known for its calming effects, aiding in the relief of sleeplessness and anxiety. The high concentration of citral in Lemon Myrtle is believed to support the immune system, and it has been used in remedies for colds, sore throats, and various digestive issues.

Cultural Significance

Lemon Myrtle has been part of Indigenous Australian culture for thousands of years, used in cooking, as a healing agent, and in ceremonial practices. Its adoption into broader Australian cuisine reflects a growing appreciation for native Australian ingredients that offer unique flavors and health benefits.

Production

Lemon Myrtle is primarily grown in Australia, where it is cultivated both for personal use in gardens and commercially for its leaves and essential oil. The tree thrives in a warm, moist climate and requires well-drained soil.

Other Facts

Lemon Myrtle is also popular in non-culinary applications, such as natural cleaning products, insect repellents, skin care, and perfumery, thanks to its strong lemon scent and antimicrobial properties.

Lemon verbena

Lemon Verbena, renowned for its strongly lemon-scented leaves, is a valued herb in culinary, medicinal, and aromatic uses. Lemon Verbena (Aloysia citrodora) is part of the Verbenaceae family and is native to South America, particularly Argentina, Chile, and Peru. It is a perennial shrub that can grow quite tall in warm climates, characterized by its lance-shaped, glossy leaves and small, pale lavender flowers. The intense lemon fragrance of its leaves, even more potent than that of actual lemons, makes lemon verbena a favorite among herbs for various applications.

Culinary Uses

Lemon Verbena's flavor is distinctly lemony, with a floral hint, making it a versatile herb in the kitchen. It is used to infuse desserts, jellies, and beverages with its bright citrus flavor. Lemon verbena can be steeped in hot water to make a refreshing herbal tea, used fresh to flavor fish, poultry, and vegetable dishes, or added to marinades and dressings. It is also an excellent addition to baked goods and can be used to make flavored syrups for cocktails or sodas. The leaves should be used sparingly due to their strong flavor, and they are often added at the end of cooking to preserve their aroma.

Medicinal Properties

Traditionally, lemon verbena has been used for its digestive and soothing properties. It is believed to help relieve indigestion, gas, and colic and has a mild sedative effect that can aid in reducing anxiety and promoting sleep. Lemon verbena is also used in weight management and to reduce inflammation due to its antioxidant properties. The essential oil extracted from the leaves is used in aromatherapy for its calming and uplifting effects.

Cultural Significance

Lemon Verbena was introduced to Europe in the 17th century and quickly became popular for its aromatic qualities and as a herbal remedy. It holds a place in traditional medicine in various cultures, especially in South America and Europe, for its health benefits. The herb is also appreciated in gardens for its decorative appearance and fragrant leaves.

Production

Lemon Verbena is cultivated in various parts of the world, especially in regions with a Mediterranean climate, including parts of Europe, North Africa, and North America (California). It thrives in full sun and well-drained soil. The plant is sensitive to cold and may require protection or to be grown in pots in cooler climates, where it can be brought indoors during winter.

Lemongrass

Lemongrass, celebrated for its citrusy scent and flavor, is a staple herb in many cuisines, particularly those of Southeast Asia, including Thai, Vietnamese, and Indonesian dishes. Lemongrass (Cymbopogon citratus) belongs to the grass family, Poaceae, and is native to tropical regions of Asia and Africa. It is a perennial plant, characterized by its tall, slender stalks and fibrous texture. Lemongrass is not only valued for its culinary uses but also for its medicinal properties and aromatic qualities.

Culinary Uses

Lemongrass's flavor is distinctly lemony, with a hint of ginger, making it a versatile ingredient in the kitchen. It is used to impart a fresh, citrus flavor to soups, curries, teas, and seafood dishes. Lemongrass is a key ingredient in many Southeast Asian dishes, such as Thai Tom Yum soup and Vietnamese Lemongrass Chicken. The lower portion of the stalk is used, which is more tender and flavorful. It can be finely chopped or bruised and added to dishes during cooking to infuse them with its flavor. Lemongrass is also commonly used in marinades and sauces to add a zesty note.

Medicinal Properties

Traditionally, lemongrass has been used for its health benefits, including its digestive, antipyretic, and analgesic properties. It is believed to help relieve stomach discomfort, reduce fever, and ease pain. Lemongrass contains citral, an essential oil that has antifungal and antibacterial properties..

Cultural Significance

Lemongrass is deeply ingrained in the culinary traditions of Southeast Asia, where it is appreciated not just for its flavor but also for its therapeutic benefits.

Production

Lemongrass is cultivated in tropical and subtropical regions around the world, with significant production in India, Thailand, Vietnam, and other parts of Southeast Asia. It grows in dense clumps that can reach up to 6 feet in height. The plant prefers full sun and well-drained soil. Lemongrass is harvested for its stalks, which are cut near the base of the plant.

Other Facts

Lemongrass is used in perfumery and aromatherapy for its refreshing and deodorizing properties. The essential oil extracted from lemongrass is widely used in soaps, candles, and insect repellents.

Lesser calamint

Lesser Calamint, known for its aromatic and minty leaves, is a versatile herb that has found its place in culinary, medicinal, and ornamental uses. Lesser Calamint (Calamintha nepeta) belongs to the mint family, Lamiaceae, and is native to Europe and the Mediterranean regions. It is a perennial herb, characterized by its small, oval-shaped leaves and clusters of delicate, lilac or white flowers. Lesser Calamint emits a pleasant, minty aroma when its leaves are bruised or crushed, contributing to its popularity in gardens and as a culinary herb.

Culinary Uses

Lesser Calamint's flavor is subtly minty with hints of oregano and thyme, making it a unique addition to various dishes. It can be used fresh or dried to season meats, fish, soups, and sauces. The herb pairs well with vegetables, particularly tomatoes and eggplants, enhancing the flavors of Mediterranean cuisine. It is also an excellent herb for infusing oils and vinegars, adding a refreshing note to dressings and marinades. Due to its potent flavor, it is advisable to use Lesser Calamint sparingly in cooking to avoid overwhelming other tastes.

Medicinal Properties

Traditionally, Lesser Calamint has been used for its digestive and soothing properties. It is believed to help relieve indigestion, gas, and mild stomach discomfort. Lesser Calamint is thought to have mild sedative effects, promoting relaxation and aiding in the treatment of insomnia.

Cultural Significance

Lesser Calamint has been cultivated and used in herbal medicine since ancient times, particularly in its native Mediterranean region. It was valued in herbalism for its aromatic qualities and its effects on the digestive system.

Production

While not as widely cultivated on a commercial scale as some other herbs, Lesser Calamint is grown in herb gardens and by specialty growers primarily in Europe. It thrives in well-drained soil and full sun, making it suitable for cultivation in a range of temperate climates. The plant is drought-resistant once established, making it a low-maintenance choice for gardeners.

Other Facts

Lesser Calamint is also popular among pollinators, attracting bees and butterflies to the garden, which contributes to the pollination of nearby plants.

Licorice (liquorice)

Licorice, known for its sweet root, is a perennial herb widely used in various culinary, medicinal, and cultural contexts around the world. Licorice (Glycyrrhiza glabra) belongs to the legume family, Fabaceae, and is native to parts of Europe and Asia, particularly the Mediterranean region, Russia, and the Middle East. It is characterized by its tall stature, reaching up to 1 meter in height, with pinnate (feather-like) leaves and small purple to whitish flowers. The root of the licorice plant is where the majority of its flavor and medicinal properties are concentrated.

Culinary Uses

Licorice's flavor is distinctively sweet, derived from the compound glycyrrhizin, which is many times sweeter than sugar. This herb is used in a variety of sweet and savory dishes, most notably in the production of licorice candy. Beyond confectionery, licorice root is used to flavor beverages, including some types of beer and soft drinks, as well as in herbal teas. It can also be used in marinades, glazes, and spice blends to add a sweet, complex flavor profile to meats and vegetables.

Medicinal Properties

Traditionally, licorice has been utilized for its health benefits, including its ability to soothe gastrointestinal problems such as acid reflux, ulcers, and inflammation of the digestive tract. Its anti-inflammatory and immune-boosting properties make it a common ingredient in herbal remedies for colds, sore throats, and respiratory issues. Licorice is also known for its adaptogenic properties, helping to manage stress and balance adrenal function.

Cultural Significance

Licorice has been valued since ancient times, with its use documented in early Egyptian, Chinese, and Greek medicines. It was traditionally used to quench thirst, alleviate hunger, and as a remedy for various ailments. In many cultures, licorice is still a symbol of sweetness and comfort, often found in traditional medicines and culinary treats.

Production

Licorice is cultivated in many parts of the world, with major producers including Italy, Greece, Turkey, and China. The plant prefers well-drained soils in full sun and requires several years of growth before the roots are harvested. After harvesting, the roots are dried, processed, and used in various forms, including whole, sliced, or powdered for culinary and medicinal purposes.

Lovage leaves

Lovage leaves, celebrated for their robust flavor, are a perennial herb that enriches a variety of dishes with their distinct taste. Lovage (Levisticum officinale) is part of the Apiaceae family, sharing kinship with parsley, carrots, and celery. It is indigenous to the Mediterranean region but has adapted well to various European and North American climates. Characterized by its tall stature, bright green leaves, and during summer, small yellow flowers, lovage is a garden herb that returns year after year.

Culinary Uses

The flavor of lovage leaves is reminiscent of celery but with a richer, more intense profile. It's a versatile herb used in European cuisines, notably in soups, stews, and salads for its ability to impart a deep, savory note. The leaves can also be chopped and used as a garnish for various dishes, offering a fresh, aromatic lift. Lovage pairs well with potatoes, tomatoes, and poultry, and its seeds can be used as a spice, similar to fennel seeds, in breads, dressings, and even cocktails for a unique flavor twist. Given its strong taste, lovage should be used sparingly to avoid overpowering other ingredients.

Medicinal Properties

The herb contains compounds that can help reduce inflammation and are believed to have diuretic effects, promoting kidney health and reducing bloating.

Cultural Significance

While lovage may not be as universally recognized as some herbs, in medieval Europe, it was highly valued both for its culinary and medicinal uses. It has a long history of cultivation in monastery gardens, where it was used for everything from flavoring dishes to treating ailments.

Production

Lovage is not as widely cultivated on a commercial scale as some other herbs, such as basil. It is more commonly found in home gardens and small-scale farms. However, its hardiness and perennial nature make it a valuable plant for those looking to maintain a sustainable herb garden. It thrives in well-drained soil and can grow quite large, providing an ample supply of leaves throughout the growing season.

Other Facts

In addition to its culinary and medicinal uses, lovage's hollow stems can be used as a straw for Bloody Marys, adding an extra layer of flavor to the drink.

Lovage seeds

Lovage seeds, derived from the plant Lovage (Levisticum officinale), are a lesser-known yet flavorful and aromatic herb that belongs to the Apiaceae family. This perennial plant is native to the Mediterranean region of Southern Europe and Asia Minor, but it has been naturalized in various parts of Europe and America. Lovage is characterized by its tall stature, reaching up to 2 meters in height, with deep green leaves and umbels of yellow flowers that bloom in early summer. The seeds, along with leaves and roots, are used for culinary and medicinal purposes.

Culinary Uses

Lovage seeds possess a flavor profile that is reminiscent of celery, with earthy and slightly bitter undertones, making them a versatile spice in the culinary world. They are commonly used in European cuisines, particularly in soups, stews, and broths, to impart a rich, aromatic depth. Additionally, lovage seeds can be found in salad dressings, marinades, and spice blends, offering a unique taste that enhances the overall flavor of dishes. They pair well with vegetables, meats, and poultry, and can be used as a natural salt substitute to add savory notes without increasing sodium content.

Medicinal Properties

Traditionally, lovage seeds have been valued for their medicinal properties, including as a diuretic to help reduce water retention and as a carminative to aid in digestion and relieve gas. The seeds contain essential oils, such as eugenol and limonene, which contribute to their therapeutic benefits. These essential oils are thought to have anti-inflammatory, antibacterial, and antifungal properties, making lovage seeds beneficial for various health concerns. Additionally, they have been used in herbal medicine to treat ailments like sore throats, menstrual discomfort, and kidney stones.

Cultural Significance

In historical contexts, lovage has been used for centuries not only as a food seasoning but also for its healing properties and in rituals. It was popular in ancient Roman and medieval European cuisines and medicine. The herb's name, derived from the Latin word "ligusticum," refers to the Liguria region in Italy, where the herb was extensively cultivated and used.

Production

Lovage is cultivated in herb gardens and commercially in various parts of Europe and the United States. It thrives in rich, moist soils in sunny to partially shaded locations. The plant is harvested for its leaves during the growing season and for its seeds and roots in late summer to autumn.

Locust beans

Locust beans, known for their distinctive flavor, are a crucial ingredient in several African cuisines, notably in West African dishes. Locust beans, derived from the seeds of the African locust bean tree (Parkia biglobosa), belong to the legume family, Fabaceae, and are native to Africa. This tree is found across the tropical savannas of West, Central, and East Africa. It is a perennial plant, characterized by its tall stature, pod-like fruits that contain the valuable seeds, and its ability to thrive in a variety of environmental conditions.

Culinary Uses

The seeds are fermented to produce a seasoning known as "dawadawa" in Hausa or "iru" in Yoruba, among other names across different cultures. This fermentation process enhances their flavor, making them a popular ingredient in soups, stews, and sauces. The unique taste of locust beans is described as rich and savory, similar to a combination of cheese and mushrooms, making it an excellent natural flavor enhancer. It is commonly used in traditional dishes such as Nigerian "egusi" soup, and it pairs well with spices, vegetables, and meats. The fermentation process not only boosts the flavor but also increases the nutritional value of the beans.

Medicinal Properties

They are rich in protein, fat, carbohydrates, and fiber, making them a nutritious addition to diets. In traditional medicine, locust beans are used to manage diabetes and hypertension and to promote digestive health.

Cultural Significance

In the cultures of West Africa, locust beans are more than just a food ingredient; they represent a link to ancestral culinary practices and sustainability. The production and fermentation process is often a communal activity, passed down through generations, emphasizing the importance of traditional knowledge and methods in food preparation.

Production

The production of locust beans is primarily in West African countries, where the climate and ecological conditions are suitable for the growth of the African locust bean tree. The harvesting of the pods, extraction of the seeds, and the fermentation process are labor-intensive tasks, typically done by hand in a traditional manner. This production method supports local economies and is integral to the cultural heritage of the regions where these trees are cultivated.

Mace

Mace, a distinguished spice derived from the nutmeg tree (Myristica fragrans), is celebrated for its warm, slightly sweet, and aromatic qualities. This spice is harvested from the reddish seed covering, or aril, that envelops the nutmeg seed. Native to the Spice Islands of Indonesia, mace has found its place in culinary traditions across the globe, particularly in European, Indian, and Middle Eastern cuisines. The nutmeg tree is unique in that it produces two distinct spices: nutmeg from the seed and mace from the seed's covering.

Culinary Uses

Mace boasts a flavor that is subtler yet similar to nutmeg, with a slightly more pungent and less sweet profile. It is a versatile spice, used in a variety of dishes ranging from savory to sweet. In European cuisine, mace is often incorporated into meat dishes, sausages, soups, and stews, as well as in spice blends like garam masala and curry powders in Indian cuisine. It lends a delicate warmth to baked goods, puddings, and custards, and is a traditional ingredient in spice cakes and pumpkin pie spice blends. Mace's compatibility with dairy makes it a preferred spice for flavoring sauces, cheese dishes, and eggnogs.

Medicinal Properties

Historically, mace has been utilized for its medicinal properties, including its use as a digestive aid, anti-inflammatory agent, and for the relief of nausea and diarrhea. It contains essential oils like myristicin and eugenol, which have been attributed with anti-inflammatory and antibacterial effects. Mace is also rich in antioxidants, which help in combating oxidative stress and may support overall health.

Cultural Significance

Mace holds cultural significance in several regions, often associated with traditional medicine and culinary heritage. In medieval Europe, it was highly valued for its culinary and preservative properties, and as a result, played a significant role in the spice trade that shaped global commerce and exploration.

Production

The leading producers of mace (and nutmeg) are Indonesia and Grenada, which is also known as the "Island of Spice." The cultivation of mace is labor-intensive, as it requires a tropical climate and the arils are removed by hand before drying. Once dried, mace turns a slightly orange or tan color and can be sold either ground or in whole pieces.

Mahleb

Mahleb, derived from the kernel of the St. Lucie cherry (Prunus mahaleb), is a cherished spice in Middle Eastern and Mediterranean cuisines. Native to the Mediterranean region and parts of Western Asia, the St. Lucie cherry tree belongs to the Rosaceae family. It is a deciduous tree, known for its fragrant white flowers and small, black cherries. The kernels of these cherries are cracked open to obtain the mahleb seeds, which are ground into a fine powder and used as a spice.

Culinary Uses

Mahleb has a unique flavor profile, offering a blend of bitter almond and cherry with subtle hints of rose and vanilla. It is predominantly used in baking and is a key ingredient in traditional recipes such as Easter breads, cookies, and pastries. In Middle Eastern cuisine, mahleb is used to flavor sweet breads, cakes, and some cheese varieties. Its distinctive taste pairs well with dairy products and enhances the flavor of baked goods, imparting a sweet, nutty aroma with a slightly fruity note.

Medicinal Properties

Traditionally, mahleb has been used in folk medicine for its perceived health benefits, including its use as a digestive aid and for relieving respiratory problems. While scientific evidence supporting these medicinal properties is limited, the spice is known to contain antioxidants and essential oils that may contribute to its health benefits.

Cultural Significance

Mahleb holds a special place in cultural and culinary traditions, particularly in the Middle East and Greece, where it is used in festive and religious baking. The spice is synonymous with celebration, often featured in recipes for holiday breads and sweets that mark significant occasions and festivals.

Production

The production of mahleb is concentrated in regions where the St. Lucie cherry tree is native. Harvesting the kernels is a labor-intensive process, as the cherries must be collected, the seeds extracted, and the kernels removed and ground. The spice is typically available in Middle Eastern and specialty food stores, sold either as whole kernels or ground powder.

Marjoram

Marjoram, a fragrant herb closely related to oregano, is a valued culinary and medicinal plant native to the Mediterranean region. Known scientifically as Origanum majorana, it belongs to the mint family, Lamiaceae, and is characterized by its sweet, citrusy, and slightly piney flavor. Marjoram is a perennial herb in its native habitat but is often grown as an annual in cooler climates. It features small, oval leaves that are gray-green in color, and during the summer, it blooms with small white or pink flowers.

Culinary Uses

The flavor of marjoram is milder and sweeter than that of oregano, with subtle hints of balsam-like pine and citrus. It is widely used in European cuisines, especially in French, Italian, and German dishes, where it enhances the taste of soups, sauces, salads, and meat preparations. Marjoram is a key ingredient in spice blends such as herbes de Provence and za'atar. Its delicate flavor pairs well with poultry, fish, vegetables, and egg dishes. Because heat can easily diminish its flavor, marjoram is often added towards the end of the cooking process or used fresh.

Medicinal Properties

Traditionally, marjoram has been employed for its numerous health benefits, including its ability to aid digestion, relieve symptoms of colds and flu, and reduce anxiety and stress. It is rich in antioxidants and has been studied for its anti-inflammatory, antimicrobial, and antiviral properties. Essential oil extracted from marjoram is used in aromatherapy and natural medicine for its calming and soothing effects.

Cultural Significance

In ancient cultures, marjoram was associated with love and happiness. It was used in wedding ceremonies and other rituals to symbolize joy and harmony. The Greeks and Romans also believed marjoram to have aphrodisiac properties.

Production

Today, marjoram is cultivated worldwide, with significant production in the Mediterranean regions, the Middle East, and North America. The herb thrives in sunny, well-drained soils and is harvested for its leaves, which are used both fresh and dried. The essential oil of marjoram, obtained through steam distillation of its leaves and flowering tops, is used in the cosmetic, pharmaceutical, and food industries.

Mastic

Mastic, a unique resin obtained from the mastic tree (Pistacia lentiscus), is a cherished ingredient native to the Mediterranean, particularly the Greek island of Chios. This evergreen shrub or small tree belongs to the pistachio family, Anacardiaceae. Mastic resin, known for its aromatic and slightly pine-like flavor, is harvested by making incisions in the tree's bark and allowing the sap to dry into translucent, yellowish tears. These tears are then collected and either used whole or ground into a powder.

Culinary Uses

Mastic's distinctive flavor is both refreshing and slightly bitter, with a hint of pine and citrus. It is a prized ingredient in Mediterranean cuisine, used in the preparation of desserts, breads, pastries, and ice creams. Mastic is also an essential component of Mastiha, a traditional Greek spirit, and is used to flavor a variety of other liqueurs and sweets across the region. In Middle Eastern cuisine, mastic is added to savory dishes, such as stews and soups, imparting a unique taste and aroma. It is particularly favored in the making of Turkish delight and various types of pudding.

Medicinal Properties

Historically, mastic has been valued for its medicinal properties, including its use as a digestive aid and for its antibacterial and antifungal benefits. It has been utilized to treat stomach ulcers, improve oral health, and support overall gastrointestinal well-being. Research has suggested that mastic resin may have antioxidant properties and potential benefits in maintaining healthy cholesterol levels and supporting liver health.

Cultural Significance

Mastic has held a significant place in culture and commerce, especially on the island of Chios, where its production is a centuries-old tradition.

Production

The production of mastic is highly localized to the southern part of Chios, The labor-intensive process of harvesting mastic, involving the careful scoring of the tree bark and collection of the resin, takes place annually during the summer months. The resin is then cleaned and sorted by hand, a process that preserves its unique qualities.

Other Facts

Mastic's ability to solidify when chewed has made it one of the earliest forms of natural chewing gum, offering fresh breath and dental health benefits.

Mint

Mint, with its refreshingly cool aroma and taste, is a widely used herb belonging to the genus Mentha within the mint family, Lamiaceae. Native to Europe, Africa, Asia, and Australia, mint has become naturalized in many parts of the world. It is a perennial herb, recognized by its square stems, small and sometimes purple or pink flowers, and vibrant green leaves. There are several varieties of mint, including peppermint (Mentha × piperita), spearmint (Mentha spicata), and apple mint (Mentha suaveolens), each offering a unique flavor profile.

Culinary Uses

Mint's cool and refreshing flavor is a favorite in cuisines globally, utilized in a myriad of dishes and beverages. It is a fundamental ingredient in Middle Eastern cuisine, used in salads, lamb dishes, and yoghurt sauces. Mint is also pivotal in the creation of mojitos, mint juleps, and other refreshing cocktails, as well as in teas, both hot and iced. In Indian cuisine, it is used in chutneys, raitas, and as a garnish for curries. Mint pairs well with fruits, desserts, chocolates, and is often used in sauces and dressings to add a fresh note to salads and meats. Its versatility extends to sweet and savory dishes, enhancing flavor profiles with its distinctive taste.

Medicinal Properties

Traditionally, mint has been valued for its medicinal properties, including its ability to aid digestion, relieve headaches, and soothe nausea or upset stomach. Peppermint oil is widely used in aromatherapy and as a natural remedy for irritable bowel syndrome (IBS), providing relief from symptoms. The menthol in mint is known for its cooling effect and is used in products aimed at relieving muscle pain, nasal congestion, and sore throats.

Cultural Significance

Mint holds a place of cultural importance in many societies. In the Middle East, serving mint tea is a sign of hospitality. In ancient times, mint was used by the Greeks and Romans for its aromatic properties, in baths, and as a room deodorizer. It has also been used historically in traditional medicines across various cultures for its therapeutic benefits.

Production

Mint is cultivated worldwide, with significant production in the United States (particularly in the Pacific Northwest), India, and parts of Europe. The herb thrives in temperate climates and can be grown both in open fields and under controlled conditions in greenhouses. Mint is harvested for its leaves, which are used fresh, dried, or distilled for essential oils and menthol.

Mountain horopito

Mountain Horopito, also known as New Zealand Pepper Tree, Horopito (Pseudowintera colorata), is an indigenous herb of New Zealand, belonging to the family Winteraceae. It is a perennial shrub, characterized by its peppery leaves that range in color from green to yellow and red, depending on the variety and season. The leaves of Horopito are adorned with red blotches, which contribute to its distinctive appearance. Unlike basil and many other herbs, Horopito does not belong to the mint family but shares a similar versatility in culinary and medicinal uses.

Culinary Uses

The flavor of Horopito is distinctly spicy and pungent, with a taste that has been compared to a blend of pepper and chili. It is used in traditional Māori cuisine and by modern New Zealand chefs to add heat and flavor to dishes. Horopito is utilized in seasoning blends, rubs for meats, and in sauces where a spicy kick is desired. Its unique flavor profile makes it suitable for gamey meats, seafood, and vegetable dishes. The leaves are typically used dried and ground into a powder, as fresh leaves can be quite tough.

Medicinal Properties

Traditionally, Horopito has been used by Māori for its medicinal properties, including as a natural remedy for fungal infections, skin conditions, and digestive issues. The active compound, polygodial, is known for its antifungal and antibacterial activity. Horopito has been researched for its potential to treat Candida overgrowth and other fungal infections, making it a valuable herb in natural medicine.

Cultural Significance

Horopito holds a significant place in Māori culture, not only as a medicinal plant but also for its use in rituals and healing practices. It is one of the oldest flowering plants, having survived for over 65 million years due to its natural antifungal and antibacterial properties, which have protected it from threats such as fungi and insects.

Production

Horopito is wild-harvested in New Zealand, thriving in its native forest environments. The plant prefers cool, shaded areas and is found throughout the country, from lowland forests to mountainous regions. Sustainable harvesting practices are essential to ensure the longevity and health of wild Horopito populations.

Musk mallow

Musk Mallow, known for its delicate flowers and musky scent, is a valued herb and ornamental plant native to Europe, Asia, and North Africa. Musk Mallow (Malva moschata) belongs to the Malvaceae family and is characterized by its soft, hairy leaves and light pink to white flowers, which bloom in the summer. It is a perennial plant, meaning it can live for more than two years, growing to heights of up to 80cm.

Culinary Uses

Though not as widely used in modern cuisine as some other herbs, the leaves and flowers of Musk Mallow are edible and have been used in traditional dishes. They can be added to salads for a delicate, slightly sweet flavor or used as a garnish. The young leaves are tender and can be eaten raw or cooked like spinach. The flowers, besides their decorative use, can also be added to desserts for their aesthetic appeal and subtle flavor.

Medicinal Properties

Historically, Musk Mallow has been valued for its medicinal properties, including its use as a mild laxative and for treating respiratory and digestive disorders. The plant contains mucilage, a gelatinous substance that can soothe irritated tissues, making it beneficial for sore throats and coughs. It also has anti-inflammatory properties and has been used in traditional medicine to treat skin conditions and wounds.

Cultural Significance

In some cultures, Musk Mallow has been associated with love and protection. It was sometimes included in bouquets or worn as a garland to attract love or ward off negative influences. The plant's musky scent was also prized in perfumery and as an aromatic herb in gardens.

Production

Musk Mallow is found growing wild in meadows, roadsides, and along hedgerows, but it is also cultivated in gardens for its ornamental value and wildlife benefits, attracting bees and butterflies with its nectar-rich flowers. It prefers well-drained soil and a sunny location. The plant is relatively low maintenance, requiring minimal care once established.

Mustard, black

Black Mustard, known for its pungent seeds, is a crucial spice in many global cuisines, especially in Indian, African, and Southern European dishes. Black Mustard (Brassica nigra) is part of the Brassicaceae family, originating from regions of Eurasia. It is an annual plant, characterized by its vibrant green leaves and small, dark brown to black seeds, which are harvested in late summer.

Culinary Uses

The flavor of Black Mustard seeds is intensely spicy and more pungent than that of its yellow mustard counterpart. They are a fundamental ingredient in Indian cooking, used in the tempering process known as tadka, where seeds are fried in oil to release their fiery flavor. These seeds are also ground into powders for mustards and spice blends, including the well-known Dijon mustard. Black Mustard seeds add a sharp heat to pickles, marinades, and curries, and are often paired with cumin, coriander, turmeric, and other spices. They must be cooked to neutralize their raw, bitter taste.

Medicinal Properties

Traditionally, Black Mustard seeds have been used for their therapeutic properties, including as a stimulant, diuretic, and to relieve muscle pain. Mustard plasters, made from the seeds, have been applied externally to treat chest congestion and inflammation. The seeds contain compounds like glucosinolates, which have been studied for their anti-cancer properties, and they are also rich in minerals such as selenium and magnesium, which have antioxidant benefits.

Cultural Significance

In various cultures, Black Mustard seeds hold symbolic meaning, often associated with faith and protection. In Christian parables, the mustard seed represents faith. In Indian traditions, they are used in rituals and ceremonies, symbolizing purity, and are often thrown into cooking fires to ward off evil spirits.

Production

India is among the largest producers of Black Mustard, followed by countries in Europe and North America. The plant thrives in temperate climates and is harvested for its seeds, which are then dried and can be used whole, cracked, or ground into powder. The oil extracted from the seeds is also used in cooking and medicinal applications.

Mustard, brown

Brown Mustard, known for its robust and spicy seeds, plays an essential role in various global cuisines, prominently in Indian, Chinese, and European cooking. Brown Mustard (Brassica juncea) is a member of the Brassicaceae family, originally from the foothills of the Himalayas. It is an annual herb, characterized by its broad, green leaves and small, reddish-brown seeds, which are harvested in late summer to early autumn.

Culinary Uses

The flavor of Brown Mustard seeds is sharp and more intense than that of yellow mustard, but slightly less pungent than black mustard seeds. They are widely used in Indian cuisine for tempering dishes and in pickling processes. Brown Mustard seeds are a key ingredient in many spice blends, including curry powders and mustards, contributing a hot and biting taste. These seeds are also used whole or ground in Chinese and European cuisines, adding depth to sauces, marinades, and dressings. The heat from the seeds is released when cracked or ground and mixed with a liquid.

Medicinal Properties

Brown Mustard seeds have been used traditionally for their medicinal properties, including as a digestive aid, in stimulating blood flow, and as an anti-inflammatory agent. Mustard plasters, made from the seeds, have been applied to the skin to relieve arthritis pain and muscle aches. The seeds contain glucosinolates, which have potential anti-cancer properties, and are rich in selenium, known for its anti-inflammatory and antioxidant effects.

Cultural Significance

In various cultures, Brown Mustard seeds are symbolic of faith, protection, and prosperity. They are used in rituals and traditional ceremonies, often symbolizing cleanliness and quickness due to their rapid germination. In some traditions, the seeds are scattered around the home to ward off evil spirits.

Production

India, Canada, and Nepal are among the leading producers of Brown Mustard, which thrives in cooler climates. The plant is harvested for its seeds, which are then dried and can be used whole, cracked, or ground into powder. Brown Mustard oil, extracted from the seeds, is also popular in cooking and medicinal applications for its strong flavor and heat.

Mustard, white

White Mustard, known for its mild and tangy seeds, is a widely used spice and condiment ingredient, particularly famous in Western cuisines. White Mustard (Sinapis alba), also known as yellow mustard, belongs to the Brassicaceae family and originates from the Mediterranean region. It is an annual plant, characterized by its bright green leaves and round, light yellow seeds, which are harvested in late summer.

Culinary Uses

The flavor of White Mustard seeds is less spicy and more subtle compared to black or brown mustard seeds, making them a popular choice for mild mustards and condiments. These seeds are the primary ingredient in American yellow mustard, appreciated for its tangy taste and vibrant color. White Mustard seeds are also used in pickling blends, salad dressings, and as a spice in various dishes, providing a gentle heat and depth of flavor. When mixed with vinegar or water, the seeds' enzymes are activated, releasing their mild spiciness and tanginess.

Medicinal Properties

Traditionally, White Mustard seeds have been used for their health benefits, including as a stimulant for digestion, to relieve muscle pains, and to improve blood circulation. Mustard plasters, created from the seeds, have been used as a home remedy to treat chest congestion by warming the chest area. The seeds contain compounds that may have anti-inflammatory and antibacterial properties, offering potential health benefits.

Cultural Significance

In many cultures, White Mustard seeds symbolize growth, fertility, and protection. They have been used in agricultural rituals and ceremonies with the belief that they bring prosperity and protect against misfortune. The seeds' mildness compared to their pungent counterparts reflects the diversity of mustard plants and their various uses in culinary and cultural practices.

Production

Canada, Nepal, and the United States are among the leading producers of White Mustard. The plant prefers temperate climates and is cultivated for its seeds, which are then dried and can be used whole, ground into powder, or processed into mustard sauce. The oil extracted from the seeds is also used in cooking and for medicinal purposes.

Mustard, yellow

Yellow Mustard, recognized for its vibrant color and mild flavor, is a fundamental condiment in many Western cuisines, particularly American. Yellow Mustard (Sinapis alba), also referred to as white mustard, is part of the Brassicaceae family, with its origins tracing back to the Mediterranean region. It is an annual plant, showcasing bright green leaves and round, yellow to light tan seeds, harvested in late summer.

Culinary Uses

The seeds of Yellow Mustard are less pungent and offer a milder taste compared to their black or brown mustard counterparts, making them the preferred choice for creating the classic American yellow mustard condiment. This condiment is a staple in hot dogs, sandwiches, and burgers for its tangy and slightly spicy flavor. Yellow Mustard seeds are also used in pickles, dressings, and as a seasoning in various dishes, providing a subtle heat and richness. When mixed with liquids, such as vinegar or water, the seeds' enzymes are activated, unleashing their characteristic mild flavor and tanginess.

Medicinal Properties

Yellow Mustard seeds have been utilized traditionally for their numerous health benefits, including as a digestive aid, for relieving muscle pain, and for enhancing blood circulation. Mustard plasters, created from ground seeds, have served as a home remedy for chest congestion by warming the chest area. These seeds are rich in compounds that may exhibit anti-inflammatory and antibacterial effects, offering potential health advantages.

Cultural Significance

In many traditions, Yellow Mustard seeds symbolize growth, fertility, and protection. They are used in agricultural rituals and ceremonies, believed to bring prosperity and protect against misfortune. The seeds' mild nature reflects the diversity within the mustard family and their various applications across culinary and cultural practices.

Production

Countries like Canada, Nepal, and the United States are leading producers of Yellow Mustard, which thrives in cooler climates. The cultivation focuses on the seeds, which are dried and can be used whole, ground into powder, or processed into mustard sauce. The oil extracted from these seeds is also employed in cooking and for medicinal purposes.

New Mexico chile

New Mexico Chile, celebrated for its unique flavor and heat, is a cornerstone of Southwestern United States cuisine, particularly in New Mexican dishes. New Mexico Chile (Capsicum annuum) is part of the nightshade family, Solanaceae, and has been cultivated in the region that is now the state of New Mexico for centuries. It comes in various types, including both green and red varieties, each with its distinct taste profile.

Culinary Uses

The flavor of New Mexico Chile ranges from mild to medium heat, characterized by its earthy and slightly fruity undertones. It is a fundamental ingredient in New Mexican cuisine, used in the preparation of the iconic red and green chile sauces that serve as a base for countless dishes, including enchiladas, burritos, and huevos rancheros. The green variety is often roasted and peeled before use, adding depth to dishes, while the dried red chiles are typically ground into a powder or rehydrated to make sauces. New Mexico Chile pairs well with meats, vegetables, and legumes, enhancing the flavors of traditional and contemporary recipes alike.

Medicinal Properties

Traditionally, New Mexico Chile has been used for its health benefits, including improving digestion, relieving pain from inflammation and arthritis, and aiding in weight loss due to its capsaicin content, which can boost metabolism.

Cultural Significance

In New Mexico, chile holds a place of pride and is deeply ingrained in the state's identity and culture. The phrase "Red or green?" is commonly asked in restaurants, referring to the diner's sauce preference, signifying the importance of chile in local cuisine. The annual Hatch Chile Festival celebrates the harvest of New Mexico Chile, drawing visitors from around the world.

Production

New Mexico is the leading producer of chile peppers in the United States, with the Hatch Valley being particularly famous for its high-quality chiles. The region's hot days and cool nights contribute to the distinct flavor profile of New Mexico Chile. The chiles are harvested in late summer and early fall, with green chiles being picked earlier in the season and red chiles left on the plant longer to mature.

Nigella sativa

Nigella sativa, commonly known as black seed or black cumin, is a highly regarded herb and spice with a rich history in culinary and medicinal uses across various cultures, notably in Middle Eastern, African, and South Asian cuisines. Nigella sativa is part of the Ranunculaceae family and is native to South and Southwest Asia. It is an annual flowering plant, characterized by its delicate blue or white flowers and distinctive black seeds, which are the main source of its culinary and health benefits.

Culinary Uses

The flavor of Nigella sativa seeds is complex and has been described as slightly bitter, peppery, and with hints of oregano and onion. They are used as a spice in breads, pastries, and curries, imparting a unique aroma and flavor to dishes. In Middle Eastern cuisines, the seeds are sprinkled on flatbreads and used in spice mixes such as panch phoron, a blend used in Bengali cooking. The seeds are also used to flavor cheeses, pickles, and salads, adding a crunchy texture and a burst of flavor. They are best when toasted lightly, which enhances their aromatic qualities.

Medicinal Properties

The seeds contain thymoquinone, an active compound believed to have antioxidant and anti-inflammatory effects. It has been used to treat various ailments, from headaches and nasal congestion to asthma and arthritis.

Cultural Significance

Nigella sativa holds a significant place in many cultures and is often referred to as the "seed of blessing" in the Islamic tradition, where it is believed to cure everything except death. Its use dates back thousands of years, with references to its healing properties found in ancient texts, including the Bible and Islamic hadiths. It has been used traditionally in various ceremonies and as a protective herb believed to ward off evil.

Production

Nigella sativa is cultivated in many countries across the Middle East, Europe, and Asia. The plant prefers arid and semi-arid climates and is harvested for its seeds, which are collected when the seed pods mature and dry. The seeds are then dried and can be used whole, ground into a powder, or pressed to extract the oil, which is also used for culinary and medicinal purposes.

Njangsa

Njangsa, also known as Djansang or Akpi, is a distinctive spice derived from the seeds of the Ricinodendron heudelotii tree, native to West and Central Africa. This tree is part of the Euphorbiaceae family and grows in tropical rainforests. Njangsa is primarily valued for its seeds, which are used as a spice or thickening agent in African cuisine.

Culinary Uses

The flavor of Njangsa seeds is nutty and slightly bitter, with a rich, earthy aroma that enhances the taste of stews, soups, and sauces. In West African cooking, particularly in Cameroon and Nigeria, Njangsa seeds are ground into a powder and added to dishes such as ndolé, soups, and fish dishes to thicken and flavor them. The seeds can also be roasted and eaten as a snack or used to extract oil, which is utilized in cooking for its distinctive flavor.

Medicinal Properties

Traditionally, Njangsa has been used in African herbal medicine for its purported health benefits, including pain relief, treatment of infertility, and as an anti-inflammatory. The seeds are believed to contain compounds that may help with stomach ailments and to promote digestion. However, scientific research on these medicinal properties is limited, and more studies are needed to confirm these health benefits.

Cultural Significance

In its native regions, Njangsa holds cultural importance not only as a culinary ingredient but also in traditional medicine and ceremonies. It is often used in local communities for its nutritional and medicinal properties, reflecting the deep connection between the people and their natural environment.

Production

Njangsa trees are widely found in the forests of West and Central Africa, with Cameroon being a notable area for Njangsa seed production. The seeds are harvested by cracking open the fruit of the Ricinodendron heudelotii tree to extract the kernel, which is then dried and can be used whole, ground into a powder, or pressed for oil.

Other Facts

Njangsa seeds are known for their unique ability to thicken and flavor dishes, making them a prized ingredient in African culinary traditions.

Nutmeg

Nutmeg, renowned for its warm, spicy flavor and aromatic fragrance, is a prized spice in culinary traditions around the globe, especially in European, Asian, and Middle Eastern cuisines. Nutmeg comes from the seed of Myristica fragrans, an evergreen tree indigenous to the Banda Islands in Indonesia, part of the spice islands. It belongs to the family Myristicaceae and is unique in that it produces two spices: nutmeg from the seed and mace from the seed covering.

Culinary Uses

Nutmeg's flavor is rich, warm, and slightly sweet, making it a versatile spice in both savory and sweet dishes. It is a key ingredient in baking, used in pies, puddings, and spice mixes such as garam masala and pumpkin spice. Nutmeg enhances the taste of sauces, soups, and vegetable dishes, and is also a classic addition to eggnog and mulled wine. Grated fresh nutmeg is preferred over pre-ground spice for its superior aroma and flavor. A little goes a long way due to its potent taste.

Medicinal Properties

Traditionally, nutmeg has been used for its medicinal properties, including as a digestive aid, to relieve pain, and to induce sleep. It contains compounds such as myristicin and eugenol, which have been studied for their antioxidant, anti-inflammatory, and antimicrobial effects. However, nutmeg should be used in moderation, as large doses can be toxic and produce adverse effects.

Cultural Significance

Nutmeg holds significant historical and cultural importance, having been a highly valuable and sought-after spice during the spice trade era, leading to the exploration of new trade routes. It symbolizes wealth and luxury in various cultures and is used in traditional ceremonies and festive cooking around the world.

Production

Today, nutmeg is cultivated in tropical regions beyond Indonesia, including Grenada, which is also known as the "Island of Spice," Sri Lanka, and the Caribbean. The nutmeg tree starts producing fruit after seven to nine years, and the seeds are harvested when the fruit splits open, revealing the bright red aril of mace surrounding the nutmeg seed.

Olida

Olida, also known as strawberry gum or forestberry herb, is a lesser-known but increasingly popular herb native to Australia. It comes from the leaves of the Eucalyptus olida tree, which is part of the Myrtaceae family. This tree is found in the forests of New South Wales and is notable for its aromatic leaves that release a strong strawberry and passion fruit scent when crushed.

Culinary Uses

The flavor of Olida is reminiscent of strawberries with a hint of passion fruit, making it a unique and versatile ingredient in both sweet and savory dishes. It is used to enhance the flavor of desserts, jams, sauces, and fruit dishes. In culinary applications, Olida can be used fresh, dried, or as an essential oil. Its sweet and fruity aroma makes it an excellent choice for flavoring baked goods, ice creams, and beverages. Chefs and food enthusiasts value Olida for its ability to add a natural berry flavor to dishes without the need for artificial additives. Olida's unique strawberry and passion fruit flavor profile make it a sought-after ingredient for innovative chefs and food producers looking to incorporate native Australian ingredients into their creations.

Medicinal Properties

While traditionally not as widely recognized for its medicinal properties as some other herbs, Olida is believed to contain antioxidant compounds due to its eucalyptus lineage. Research into its specific health benefits is ongoing, but it is thought to share some of the antimicrobial and anti-inflammatory properties of other eucalyptus species.

Cultural Significance

Olida, like many Australian native herbs and spices, is part of the broader Australian bush food tradition, which is gaining recognition and appreciation both domestically and internationally. Its use highlights the rich biodiversity of Australia's flora and the growing interest in sustainable and native ingredients in culinary practices.

Production

The cultivation and production of Olida are limited compared to more widely known herbs, primarily due to its native growth in specific regions of Australia. However, with the increasing interest in native Australian ingredients, there are efforts to cultivate Olida more broadly for culinary use. It is harvested for its leaves, which are then dried or distilled into essential oil.

Oregano

Oregano, celebrated for its pungent and peppery flavor, is a fundamental herb in Mediterranean and Mexican cuisines. Oregano (Origanum vulgare) belongs to the mint family, Lamiaceae, and is native to the warm climates of Eurasia and the Mediterranean region. It is a perennial herb, known for its aromatic, oval leaves and purple flowers. There are several varieties of oregano, each with a unique flavor profile, including Greek oregano, Italian oregano, and Mexican oregano, which actually comes from a different plant family but shares a similar flavor profile.

Culinary Uses

Oregano's flavor is robust, with earthy and somewhat bitter notes, making it an essential ingredient in Italian dishes such as pizza, pasta sauces, and grilled meats. It is also a staple in Greek cuisine, used in salads, dressings, and marinades. Mexican oregano, on the other hand, adds depth to chili powders, beans, and salsas. Oregano pairs well with tomatoes, garlic, lemon, and olive oil. Its leaves can be used fresh or dried, but the dried form tends to have a more concentrated flavor. It is best added during the cooking process to allow its flavors to meld with the dish.

Medicinal Properties

Traditionally, oregano has been used for its medicinal properties, including its ability to treat respiratory tract disorders, gastrointestinal (GI) disorders, and menstrual cramps. Oregano contains compounds such as thymol and carvacrol, which have been studied for their antibacterial and anti-inflammatory properties. It is also rich in antioxidants, which can help protect against oxidative stress and support the immune system.

Cultural Significance

Oregano has a rich history in Mediterranean cultures, where it has been used for thousands of years, not only as a culinary herb but also for its health benefits. It was believed to bring happiness and protection, and it was often planted around homes for these reasons. In Greek mythology, oregano was a symbol of joy and was used to crown brides and grooms.

Production

Today, oregano is cultivated worldwide, with major producers including Italy, Turkey, and Mexico. The herb thrives in climates with hot, dry summers. It is harvested just before the plant flowers when its leaves contain the highest concentration of essential oils, which contribute to its distinctive flavor.

Oregano, Cuban

Cuban Oregano, also known as Plectranthus amboinicus, is a perennial herb notable for its aromatic and succulent leaves, widely used in tropical regions for both culinary and medicinal purposes. Despite its common name, Cuban Oregano is not a true oregano in the botanical sense but is closely related to the mint family, Lamiaceae. It is native to Southern and Eastern Africa but has become naturalized in other tropical regions, including the Caribbean and parts of Asia. The plant is characterized by its thick, fuzzy leaves, with a strong, pungent aroma reminiscent of oregano and thyme.

Culinary Uses

Cuban Oregano's flavor is intense and robust, making it a popular herb in Caribbean, Indian, and Southeast Asian cuisines. Its leaves are used sparingly in cooking due to their strong flavor. They can be added to stews, soups, marinades, and meat dishes to impart a deep, aromatic taste. The herb is particularly well-suited for heavy and rich dishes, where it can stand up to other bold flavors. Fresh leaves are preferred in cooking, as they offer a more potent flavor than dried ones.

Medicinal Properties

Traditionally, Cuban Oregano has been utilized for its medicinal benefits, including treating respiratory conditions, digestive problems, and as an antiseptic for minor cuts and bruises. The leaves contain essential oils with antimicrobial and anti-inflammatory properties, making them useful in traditional medicine to alleviate symptoms of coughs, colds, and sore throats.

Cultural Significance

In regions where Cuban Oregano is grown, it is often found in home gardens and used in traditional home remedies. Its ease of cultivation and propagation, along with its medicinal uses, have made it a valuable plant in many households in tropical climates.

Production

Cuban Oregano thrives in warm, humid environments and is often grown in containers or gardens where it can receive ample sunlight. It is a hardy plant that requires minimal care, making it accessible to gardeners of all skill levels. The plant can be easily propagated from cuttings, allowing for widespread cultivation without the need for seeds.

Oregano, Greek

Greek Oregano, renowned for its bold and peppery flavor, is an essential herb in Greek and Mediterranean cuisines. Greek Oregano (Origanum vulgare subsp. hirtum) is a subspecies of the common oregano and belongs to the mint family, Lamiaceae. It is native to Greece and the Mediterranean region, where it grows wild on the mountainous slopes, thriving in the warm and dry climate. This perennial herb is characterized by its small, round, and dark green leaves, and delicate purple flowers.

Culinary Uses

Greek Oregano is distinguished from other varieties by its earthy and aromatic qualities, making it a staple in Mediterranean cooking. Greek Oregano's flavor is more intense and less bitter than that of common oregano, making it a favorite among chefs and home cooks alike. It is widely used in Greek dishes such as salads, grilled meats, and sauces, imparting a depth of flavor that is synonymous with Mediterranean cooking. It is also a key ingredient in Italian cuisine, especially in tomato-based pasta sauces, pizza, and seasoning for meats and vegetables. The herb pairs well with lemon, garlic, olive oil, and tomatoes, and it is best added towards the end of cooking to preserve its essential oils and vibrant taste.

Medicinal Properties

Traditionally, Greek Oregano has been used for its ability to fight bacteria, relieve inflammation, and soothe digestive issues. It is rich in antioxidants and compounds like thymol and carvacrol, which have been studied for their antimicrobial and anti-inflammatory effects.

Cultural Significance

In Greek culture, oregano is more than just a culinary herb; it is a symbol of joy and happiness. It was believed that cows that grazed on fields of oregano would produce tastier meat. Oregano is also used in traditional Greek weddings and is often found in home gardens, reflecting its deep-rooted significance in Greek lifestyle and cuisine.

Production

Greece remains a leading producer of Greek Oregano, along with other Mediterranean countries. The herb is cultivated for its leaves, which are harvested just before the plant flowers when the concentration of essential oils is at its peak. Greek Oregano is available fresh or dried, with the dried form being more common due to its concentrated flavor and longer shelf life.

Orris root

Orris Root, derived from the rhizomes of Iris germanica, Iris pallida, and Iris florentina, is a valued herb traditionally used in perfumery, medicine, and as a flavoring agent. It belongs to the Iridaceae family and is native to the Mediterranean region and Morocco. Orris Root undergoes a lengthy drying process, often taking several years, which allows its characteristic scent and flavor to develop—a fragrance reminiscent of violets and a flavor that is slightly sweet and floral.

Culinary Uses

While not as commonly used in modern cuisine, Orris Root has historical culinary applications, primarily as a flavoring agent in spirits and syrups. It imparts a subtle floral note and is sometimes used in the production of gin and other flavored spirits. Additionally, it has been utilized in traditional European cuisine for flavoring certain sweets and baked goods.

Medicinal Properties

Orris Root has been used as a diuretic, to treat coughs and bronchial problems, and for its anti-inflammatory effects. Its essence, orris oil, extracted through steam distillation of the dried roots, has been employed in herbal medicine to address dental issues, skin conditions, and for detoxification.

Cultural Significance

In historical contexts, Orris Root held significant cultural importance, particularly in perfumery and cosmetics, due to its unique violet-like fragrance. It was also used in potpourri and sachets to scent linens and clothing. The root was believed to have protective qualities and was sometimes used in talismans and charms.

Production

The cultivation of Iris species for Orris Root primarily occurs in Italy, Morocco, and other parts of the Mediterranean. The harvesting process involves collecting the rhizomes of plants that are at least two to three years old. After harvesting, the roots are cleaned, peeled, and then left to dry for as long as five years. This drying process is crucial for developing the root's flavor.

Other Facts

Orris Root powder is also used in natural dentistry as a toothpaste ingredient for its mild abrasive properties and pleasant scent. In the perfume industry, orris root is highly prized for its fixative properties, helping to stabilize the scent of natural perfumes.

Pandan flower

Pandan Flower, derived from the Pandanus plant, is a tropical herb known for its aromatic and floral scent, playing a significant role in Southeast Asian culinary traditions. While the leaves of the Pandanus amaryllifolius are more commonly used for their flavor and aroma, the flowers of certain Pandanus species also contribute unique scents and flavors to dishes and are valued in traditional ceremonies.

Culinary Uses

The essence of Pandan Flower is often extracted and used as a flavoring in desserts, cakes, and sweet beverages, imparting a subtle, floral sweetness that is highly sought after in many Asian cuisines. In some traditions, the flowers themselves may be used to infuse rice dishes, teas, or syrups, adding a distinct and delicate fragrance. The aromatic property of Pandan is sometimes compared to vanilla, with its own unique nuance, making it a favorite ingredient in rice dishes like kaya (a type of coconut jam) and various sweet snacks.

Medicinal Properties

Though the leaves are more commonly associated with medicinal benefits, Pandan in general, including its flowers, is believed to have health benefits such as pain relief, reduction of fever, and treatment of certain health conditions. The plant is rich in essential oils, flavonoids, and other compounds that have been studied for their potential antioxidant and anti-inflammatory properties.

Cultural Significance

Pandan is deeply ingrained in the cultures of Southeast Asia, not only for its culinary uses but also for its role in rituals and traditional practices. The sweet fragrance of Pandan Flowers is sometimes used in religious ceremonies, weddings, and other celebrations as a natural perfume or air freshener, symbolizing purity and elegance.

Production

Pandan is native to Southeast Asia and thrives in tropical climates. While the plant is widely cultivated for its leaves, the flowers are less commonly harvested but are still an integral part of the plant's overall value. The cultivation of Pandan primarily focuses on areas with ample water and humidity, reflecting the plant's natural habitat in regions like Indonesia, Malaysia, Thailand, and the Philippines.

Pandan leaf

Pandan Leaf, celebrated for its unique sweet and fragrant aroma, is a crucial ingredient in Southeast Asian cooking, akin to how vanilla is used in Western cuisines. Derived from the Pandanus amaryllifolius plant, it belongs to the Pandanaceae family and is native to tropical regions of Asia. The plant is characterized by its long, narrow, and blade-like green leaves, which are used both fresh and dried to impart flavor and color to a variety of dishes.

Culinary Uses

The sweet, floral flavor of Pandan Leaf is versatile, making it a staple in a myriad of dishes ranging from savory rice and curries to sweet desserts and drinks. It is commonly used to wrap meats and fish before cooking, infusing them with its distinctive aroma. In desserts, Pandan Leaves are used to flavor cakes, jellies, and sweet beverages. They are also boiled to make a fragrant extract that colors food naturally with a vibrant green hue. The leaves can be woven into baskets for steaming food, adding a subtle fragrance during the cooking process.

Medicinal Properties

Traditionally, Pandan Leaves have been used in herbal medicine for their pain-relieving, anti-inflammatory, and anti-anxiety properties. They are also used as a natural air freshener and insect repellent due to their pleasant scent.

Cultural Significance

In Southeast Asia, Pandan Leaves hold a significant cultural value, often associated with good fortune and used in ceremonial offerings. Their use spans from culinary applications to traditional rituals, symbolizing the deep connection between the people and their natural environment.

Production

Pandan Leaves are widely cultivated in home gardens and farms throughout Southeast Asia, including countries like Thailand, Malaysia, Indonesia, and the Philippines. The plant thrives in humid, tropical climates and requires minimal maintenance, making it accessible to a broad range of growers.

Other Facts

Pandan Leaves are not only prized for their aroma and flavor but also for their natural coloring properties, which offer a chemical-free alternative to artificial food colorings.

Pápalo

Pápalo, a distinctive herb native to Central and South America, is celebrated for its bold, complex flavor, often compared to a mix of cilantro, arugula, and rue. It belongs to the family Asteraceae and is known scientifically as Porophyllum ruderale or Porophyllum tagetoides. Papalo is an annual herb, characterized by its broad, round, blue-green leaves and a potent aroma that intensifies when the leaves are crushed.

Culinary Uses

Papalo's unique flavor is a staple in traditional Mexican and South American cuisines, where it is used raw, added to dishes just before serving to preserve its intense aroma and taste. It is commonly found in sandwiches, salads, salsas, and as a topping for tacos and guacamole. Due to its strong flavor, it is used sparingly and often as a substitute for cilantro in dishes for those who prefer its more robust taste.

Medicinal Properties

Traditionally, Papalo has been used in herbal medicine for various purposes, including as a diuretic, for treating high blood pressure, and for stomach disorders. Its antibacterial properties have also been recognized in traditional practices, although scientific research is limited.

Cultural Significance

In its native regions, Papalo is not just a culinary herb but also a plant with significant cultural importance. It is often grown in home gardens and used in traditional dishes, reflecting a deep connection to local food traditions and natural remedies.

Production

Papalo is cultivated primarily in Mexico, Bolivia, and other parts of Central and South America. The herb is typically harvested fresh and used immediately to take advantage of its potent flavor and aroma.

Other Facts

Unlike many herbs, Papalo does not dry well and is best enjoyed fresh. Its powerful flavor can be overwhelming, so it is recommended to start with a small amount and adjust to taste. Papalo is sometimes referred to as "summer cilantro" because it thrives in hot weather, making it an excellent cilantro substitute for summer dishes when cilantro may bolt and lose its flavor.

Paprika

Paprika, celebrated for its vibrant color and sweet to smoky flavor, is a versatile spice made from ground bell peppers and chili peppers, belonging to the Capsicum annuum species. Originating from the Americas but extensively used and produced in Hungary, Spain, and other parts of the world, paprika has become a staple in various cuisines. It is available in several varieties, including sweet, smoked, and hot, each offering a unique flavor profile and culinary application.

Culinary Uses

Paprika's rich color and flavor make it a popular ingredient in a wide range of dishes. It is a key component in Hungarian cuisine, famously used in goulash and chicken paprikash. In Spanish cooking, smoked paprika, or pimentón, adds depth to chorizo, paella, and tapas dishes. Sweet paprika is often used as a garnish for potatoes, soups, and salads, while the hotter varieties spice up stews, rice dishes, and marinades. Paprika pairs well with meats, vegetables, and legumes, enhancing dishes with its warm, earthy tones.

Medicinal Properties

Paprika is rich in vitamins A and C, antioxidants, and capsaicin in its hotter forms, which have been studied for their health benefits. These include improving eye health, reducing inflammation, and potentially having anti-cancer properties. The spice is also known to boost metabolism, aiding in weight loss and digestive health.

Cultural Significance

Paprika holds a place of pride in Hungarian and Spanish cultures, symbolizing the rich culinary heritage and traditional farming practices in these regions. It is celebrated in festivals and considered a national treasure, especially in Hungary, where the spice is deeply embedded in the nation's identity and culinary traditions.

Production

Hungary and Spain are among the leading producers of paprika, with each country offering varieties unique to its climate and soil conditions. The peppers are harvested, dried, and then ground into a fine powder. The process varies by region and desired flavor, with some types being smoked over wood fires to achieve a distinct smoky aroma and taste.

Paracress

Paracress, also known as Spilanthes acmella, is a flowering herb recognized for its unique tingling and numbing sensation upon consumption. Native to the tropics of Brazil, it belongs to the Asteraceae family and has spread to various tropical and subtropical regions worldwide. It is an annual herb, characterized by its bronzy-green, spindle-shaped leaves and distinctive gold and red flower heads, which are the primary source of its culinary and medicinal properties.

Culinary Uses

The flavor of Paracress is pungent and has a powerful numbing effect, akin to that of Sichuan peppercorns, earning it the nickname "toothache plant." It is used sparingly in salads, as a garnish, or in traditional dishes to add a unique burst of flavor and sensation. The leaves and flowers can be chewed fresh or added to foods for their surprising effect and to stimulate the salivary glands, enhancing the taste of other ingredients.

Medicinal Properties

Traditionally, Paracress has been utilized for its analgesic properties to treat toothaches and gum infections, owing to its ability to numb the mouth and relieve pain. It contains compounds such as spilanthol, which have been studied for their anti-inflammatory, antimicrobial, and analgesic effects. The herb is also used in traditional medicine to aid digestion and improve oral health.

Cultural Significance

In regions where Paracress is native or has been naturalized, it is not only valued for its culinary uniqueness but also for its medicinal benefits. It is commonly found in home gardens and used in traditional remedies, reflecting its integration into local health practices and cuisines.

Production

Paracress is cultivated in tropical and subtropical gardens for its edible and medicinal parts. It thrives in warm, moist conditions and can be grown from seeds or cuttings. The plant is harvested for its leaves and flowers, which are used fresh to maximize their potent effects.

Other Facts

Due to its strong, numbing sensation, Paracress is often used in small amounts. It is also being explored for its potential in natural dental care products, such as mouthwashes and toothpaste.

Parsley

Parsley, a versatile and widely used herb, is a staple in many cuisines around the globe, including European, Middle Eastern, and American dishes. Parsley (Petroselinum crispum) belongs to the Apiaceae family and is native to the central Mediterranean region (southern Italy, Greece, Portugal, Spain, Malta, Morocco, Algeria, and Tunisia). It is a biennial plant in temperate climates but is often cultivated as an annual. Characterized by its bright green leaves, parsley comes in two main varieties: flat-leaf (Italian) parsley, with its robust flavor, and curly leaf parsley, which is milder and often used as a garnish.

Culinary Uses

Parsley's flavor is fresh and slightly peppery, with clean and crisp notes. It is a key ingredient in dishes such as tabbouleh, soups, stews, sauces, and salads. Italian parsley, with its more intense flavor, is preferred in cooking, while curly parsley is frequently used as a decorative garnish. Parsley pairs well with a wide range of foods, including potatoes, tomatoes, poultry, beef, seafood, and other herbs like basil and rosemary. It is best added towards the end of cooking or as a garnish to preserve its vibrant color and flavor.

Medicinal Properties

Traditionally, parsley has been used for its digestive and diuretic properties. It is rich in vitamins A, C, and K, as well as flavonoids and antioxidants, which can help to boost the immune system, protect against free radical damage, and support bone health. Parsley is also known for its ability to freshen breath, particularly after consuming garlic.

Cultural Significance

Parsley is more than just a culinary herb; it has been used in various cultural and ceremonial contexts for centuries. In some traditions, it is associated with death and is used at funerals, while in others, it symbolizes spring and renewal. Parsley is also a symbol of festivity in some cultures, used to decorate and flavor holiday dishes.

Production

Parsley is cultivated worldwide, with major producers including the United States, parts of Europe, and the Mediterranean region. It thrives in full sun to partial shade and prefers moist, well-drained soil. The herb is harvested for its leaves, which can be used fresh or dried for later use.

Other Facts

Parsley is not only a culinary herb but also a source of essential oil, used in the cosmetic and pharmaceutical industries.

Pennyroyal

Pennyroyal, known scientifically as Mentha pulegium, is a perennial herb in the mint family, Lamiaceae, native to Europe, North Africa, and the Middle East. It has a strong, minty aroma and flavor, characterized by its small, round leaves and lilac flowers. Historically, it has been used for culinary, medicinal, and aromatic purposes, though its use in cooking is now less common due to its potent nature.

Culinary Uses

Traditionally, pennyroyal was used in small amounts to flavor various dishes, including sauces, soups, and teas. Its intense minty flavor was prized in medieval cuisine, but due to its strong taste and potential toxicity, it is seldom used in modern cooking. When used, it is typically in herbal tea blends, and care is taken to use it sparingly.

Medicinal Properties

Pennyroyal has been known for its medicinal properties, including its use as a digestive aid, antiseptic, and for its ability to induce sweating. It has also been used traditionally as an insect repellent and for inducing menstruation. However, due to its high pulegone content, which can be toxic and potentially lethal if ingested in large quantities, its medicinal use is now largely discouraged without professional guidance.

Cultural Significance

In ancient cultures, pennyroyal was used for its aromatic properties in cooking and for warding off pests. It was also believed to purify water and air, making it a common herb in household practices for promoting health and cleanliness.

Production

Pennyroyal is found growing wild in its native habitats and can be cultivated in temperate garden settings. It thrives in moist, well-drained soil in full sun to partial shade. The plant is harvested for its leaves and flowering tops, which are used fresh or dried for herbal preparations.

Other Facts

Due to its potential toxicity, pennyroyal oil, especially, should be used with extreme caution and never ingested. The herb itself should only be used under the guidance of a qualified healthcare provider. Despite its historical uses, the risks associated with pennyroyal now limit its application.

Pepper

Pepper, known as the "king of spices," is an essential spice in cuisines around the globe, derived from the berries of the Piper nigrum vine, belonging to the Piperaceae family. Native to the Western Ghats of Kerala in India, pepper has played a pivotal role in history, driving exploration and trade. It is available in various forms, including black, white, green, and red pepper, each with its unique flavor profile and culinary application.

Culinary Uses

Pepper's flavor is pungent and mildly spicy, with black pepper being the most common, characterized by its sharp, warming taste. It is a versatile spice used in seasoning blends, marinades, sauces, and as a table condiment. Black pepper enhances the flavor of meats, vegetables, and salads. White pepper, with its milder taste, is preferred in European cuisine for light-colored dishes. Green and red peppercorns are used in fresh or pickled form, adding a bright, zesty flavor to dishes.

Medicinal Properties

Traditionally, pepper has been valued for its digestive stimulant properties. It contains piperine, which has been studied for its potential to enhance nutrient absorption, improve digestion, and possess anti-inflammatory and antioxidant effects. Pepper is also believed to have antimicrobial properties, contributing to food preservation.

Cultural Significance

Pepper has a rich history, symbolizing wealth and prosperity. It was a luxury item in ancient Rome and a driving force behind the spice trade in the Middle Ages. Its importance in global trade routes has significantly impacted world history, leading to the discovery of new continents.

Production

India, Vietnam, Brazil, and Indonesia are among the leading producers of pepper. The Piper nigrum vine thrives in tropical climates with rich, well-drained soil. The berries are harvested at various stages of ripeness and processed differently to produce black, white, green, and red peppercorns.

Pepper, Brazilian

The term "Brazilian pepper" typically refers to the plant Schinus terebinthifolia, also known as the Brazilian peppertree, aroeira, rose pepper, and broadleaved pepper tree. It is not a true pepper (Piper nigrum) but belongs to the family Anacardiaceae. Native to subtropical and tropical South America, Brazilian pepper has become an invasive species in various regions, including Florida, Texas, and California in the United States.

Culinary Uses

While not as commonly used in cuisine as other spices, the pink peppercorns harvested from the Brazilian peppertree can be used to add a mild pepper flavor with hints of sweetness to dishes. They are often used as a garnish or ingredient in salads, meats, and seafood dishes, imparting a unique flavor and decorative appearance. However, it's important to note that while they are used in gourmet cooking, there are concerns about potential allergic reactions in some individuals, as the plant is related to the cashew and mango trees, which are known allergens.

Medicinal Properties

Traditionally, various parts of the Brazilian peppertree have been used in folk medicine in its native range for treating a range of ailments, including wounds, arthritis, and gastrointestinal issues. The plant contains compounds that have been studied for their anti-inflammatory and antimicrobial properties. However, its medicinal use should be approached with caution due to the risk of allergic reactions.

Cultural Significance

In South America, the Brazilian peppertree holds cultural significance for its medicinal and symbolic uses. However, in places where it has been introduced and become invasive, it is often viewed as a pest due to its aggressive growth and impact on local ecosystems.

Production

Originally from South America, Brazilian pepper has been introduced to other parts of the world, both as an ornamental plant and unintentionally. In areas where it is considered invasive, control measures are often implemented to manage its spread. The plant thrives in a range of environmental conditions, which has contributed to its invasive status outside its native range.

Pepper, Dorrigo

Dorrigo pepper (Tasmannia stipitata), native to the subtropical rainforests of Eastern Australia, particularly in areas around Dorrigo and northern New South Wales, is a unique and aromatic herb. It belongs to the Winteraceae family, distinct from the more commonly known pepper varieties such as black or white pepper (Piper nigrum). Dorrigo pepper is characterized by its dark green leaves and deep purple berries, which are harvested for their spicy, complex flavor profile.

Culinary Uses

Dorrigo pepper's leaves and dried berries are used to impart a robust, peppery flavor with hints of herbal and floral notes to dishes. It is particularly favored in Australian cuisine for seasoning meats, sauces, and marinades, adding a unique depth and warmth. The spice is known for its ability to retain its flavor even when cooked at high temperatures, making it versatile for both savory and sweet dishes. Its berries are often ground into a powder and used as a more potent and aromatic alternative to traditional black pepper.

Medicinal Properties

Traditionally, Dorrigo pepper has been valued for its medicinal properties, including its use as an antioxidant and anti-inflammatory agent. The plant contains polygodal, a compound that has been studied for its potential to soothe digestive ailments and stimulate the immune system. Its antibacterial properties also make it a natural preservative and a beneficial addition to a healthy diet.

Cultural Significance

While not as widely recognized in global cuisine, Dorrigo pepper holds cultural significance in Australia, particularly within indigenous communities and among chefs and food enthusiasts exploring native Australian ingredients. Its use symbolizes a growing appreciation for local, sustainable, and underutilized native plants.

Production

Dorrigo pepper is harvested from wild populations and increasingly cultivated in specialty gardens and small-scale farms focused on native Australian plants. The cool, moist climate of its native habitat is essential for its growth, making it a specialty crop outside of its natural range. The leaves are typically harvested throughout the year, while the berries are collected in autumn when they are ripe.

Pepper, long

Long pepper, scientifically known as Piper longum, is a spice that originates from the same family as black and white pepper, the Piperaceae. Native to India, long pepper was once a widely used spice in ancient Rome and Greece but has since been overshadowed by its cousin, black pepper (Piper nigrum). It is characterized by its long, slender, catkin-like appearance, which is composed of many tiny fruits embedded in a spike.

Culinary Uses

Long pepper's flavor is more complex than that of black pepper, with a sweetly spicy heat and hints of cinnamon, cardamom, and ginger. It is used in Indian, Indonesian, and Malaysian cuisines, among others, to season pickles, curries, and spicy dishes. Long pepper can be ground into powders or used whole in slow-cooked recipes, where its full flavor profile can infuse the dish. It pairs well with other aromatic spices and is an essential component of certain spice blends, such as garam masala in Indian cuisine and certain Indonesian spice pastes.

Medicinal Properties

Traditionally, long pepper has been used in Ayurvedic medicine for its therapeutic properties, including enhancing digestion, treating respiratory infections, and improving metabolism. It contains piperine, the same active compound found in black pepper, which is known for its ability to increase the absorption of nutrients and medications in the body. Additionally, long pepper has been studied for its anti-inflammatory and analgesic effects.

Cultural Significance

In ancient times, long pepper held significant value in trade and was considered a luxury spice in Europe, contributing to the spice trade's expansion. It has been used in traditional medicine systems in Asia for thousands of years, underscoring its importance in both culinary and medicinal practices.

Production

Long pepper is primarily cultivated in India, Indonesia, and Malaysia. It thrives in tropical climates and is harvested by hand. The spice is typically dried before use, which concentrates its flavors and allows for longer storage. Despite its decline in popularity in the West, long pepper continues to be a valued spice in its native regions and among gourmet chefs and culinary enthusiasts worldwide.

Pepper, mountain

Mountain Pepper, known scientifically as Tasmannia lanceolata, is a unique herb and spice native to the cool temperate rainforests of Tasmania, Australia. Belonging to the Winteraceae family, Mountain Pepper is characterized by its dark green leaves and deep purple-black berries. This perennial shrub is highly valued for both its leaves and berries, which are used in culinary applications for their spicy, peppery flavor with hints of Australian bush.

Culinary Uses

Mountain Pepper's leaves and dried berries are used to impart a robust, aromatic flavor to a variety of dishes. The leaves can be used fresh or dried and ground into a powder, similar to how traditional black pepper is used. They are excellent for seasoning meats, soups, and sauces, offering a distinctive peppery taste with a slightly herbal note. The berries, which are more potent than the leaves, add depth to marinades, chutneys, and spice blends. Mountain Pepper is celebrated in Australian cuisine for its ability to enhance the flavors of game meats, seafood, and vegetarian dishes, adding a unique twist to traditional recipes.

Medicinal Properties

Traditionally, Mountain Pepper has been used by Indigenous Australians for its medicinal properties, including treating stomach ailments and skin disorders. The plant is rich in antioxidants, particularly polyphenolic compounds, which contribute to its anti-inflammatory and antimicrobial benefits.

Cultural Significance

Mountain Pepper holds cultural significance in Australia, especially among Indigenous communities who have used the plant for centuries as part of their traditional food and medicine. It represents the rich biodiversity of Australian flora and the growing interest in native Australian ingredients among chefs and food enthusiasts worldwide.

Production

Mountain Pepper is primarily harvested in the wild, though it is increasingly being cultivated commercially as demand for native Australian spices grows. Sustainable harvesting practices are essential to ensure the conservation of wild populations. The plant thrives in cool, moist conditions typical of the Tasmanian wilderness and requires specific care when cultivated outside its natural habitat.

Peppermint

Peppermint, a highly aromatic herb, is a staple in both culinary and medicinal contexts worldwide. Peppermint (Mentha × piperita) is a hybrid mint, a cross between watermint (Mentha aquatica) and spearmint (Mentha spicata), belonging to the mint family, Lamiaceae. It is a perennial herb, characterized by its smooth, square stems, dark green leaves, and purple-tinged flowers. The distinct, refreshing aroma and cooling effect of peppermint are due to its high menthol content.

Culinary Uses

Peppermint's bold, refreshing flavor makes it a popular ingredient in a variety of dishes and beverages. It is widely used in teas, cocktails, and mocktails for its cooling sensation. Peppermint enhances the taste of chocolates, desserts, and confectioneries, and is also used in sauces and dressings. Fresh or dried peppermint leaves can be used in salads, adding a fresh, zesty flavor. Its extract is a key component in flavoring gum, toothpaste, and other minty products.

Medicinal Properties

Traditionally, peppermint has been used for its numerous health benefits. It is well-known for its ability to soothe digestive issues, such as indigestion, gas, and irritable bowel syndrome (IBS). The menthol in peppermint helps relieve congestion and symptoms of colds and coughs. Peppermint oil is used in aromatherapy to reduce stress and improve mental clarity. Its analgesic properties make it useful in alleviating headaches and muscle pain.

Cultural Significance

Peppermint has been cultivated for thousands of years and holds significance in various cultures for its medicinal and culinary uses. It is commonly used in holiday treats and beverages, symbolizing celebration and freshness. Peppermint's widespread use in traditional remedies across cultures underscores its value as a natural healing agent.

Production

Peppermint is cultivated in many parts of the world, with major producers including the United States, India, and parts of Europe. The plant prefers a moist, shaded environment and fertile, well-drained soil. It is harvested just before flowering for optimal oil content. Peppermint leaves are used fresh, dried, or distilled to extract essential oil, which is a key ingredient in many health and beauty products.

Peppermint gum leaf

Peppermint Gum Leaf, derived from the Eucalyptus dives species, is a native Australian herb known for its strong peppermint scent and flavor. It belongs to the Myrtaceae family and is characterized by its broad, aromatic leaves which contain high levels of essential oils. Unlike traditional peppermint, Peppermint Gum Leaf comes from a type of eucalyptus tree, showcasing the diverse flora of Australia.

Culinary Uses

The intense peppermint flavor of Peppermint Gum Leaf makes it a unique and refreshing ingredient in culinary applications. It can be used to infuse desserts, teas, and cocktails with a minty aroma, as well as in sauces and dressings to add a burst of freshness. The leaves can also be used as a garnish or incorporated into spice rubs and marinades for meats, offering a distinctive Australian twist to traditional dishes.

Medicinal Properties

Traditionally, Peppermint Gum Leaf has been used in Australian Aboriginal medicine for its antiseptic and respiratory benefits. The essential oils in the leaves, particularly eucalyptol, are valued for their ability to clear congestion, ease breathing, and soothe coughs. Additionally, the antimicrobial properties of the leaf make it useful in treating wounds and skin infections.

Cultural Significance

Peppermint Gum Leaf holds cultural significance in Australia, representing the country's rich botanical heritage and the traditional uses of native plants by Aboriginal Australians. It is increasingly celebrated in contemporary Australian cuisine for its unique flavor and as a symbol of the growing interest in indigenous ingredients and sustainable foraging.

Production

Peppermint Gum Leaf is harvested from the Eucalyptus dives trees, which are found in the cooler regions of southeastern Australia. The leaves are collected for their essential oils, which are extracted and used in various applications, including culinary, medicinal, and aromatic products. Sustainable harvesting practices are important to ensure the preservation of this native species and its habitat.

Perilla

Perilla, known for its distinctive aroma and flavor, is an essential herb in Korean, Japanese, and Vietnamese cuisines. Perilla (Perilla frutescens) belongs to the mint family, Lamiaceae, and is native to Southeast Asia and the Indian highlands. It is an annual herb, characterized by its broad, round leaves that can vary in color from green to purple, depending on the variety. Perilla is often referred to as Korean perilla, Japanese shiso, or Vietnamese tía tô, each with its unique flavor profile and culinary uses.

Culinary Uses

Perilla's flavor is complex, described as a combination of mint, basil, cinnamon, and anise, with a slightly spicy undertone. It is used extensively in Asian cuisine for wrapping meat, in salads, as a garnish, and in pickled dishes. The leaves can be fried, grilled, or used fresh, adding depth and a burst of flavor to a variety of dishes. In Korea, perilla leaves are often marinated and served as a side dish, while in Japan, the red variety (shiso) is used to color and flavor umeboshi (pickled plums) and to garnish sashimi. Perilla seeds are also used to make oil, which is utilized in cooking for its nutty flavor.

Medicinal Properties

Traditionally, perilla has been used for its supposed health benefits, including anti-inflammatory and antioxidant properties. It is believed to help with asthma, relieve indigestion, and boost the immune system. The leaves contain rosmarinic acid, which has been studied for its potential to reduce allergic reactions and improve overall health.

Cultural Significance

Perilla holds a significant place in Asian cultures, not only for its culinary uses but also for its medicinal properties. It is commonly grown in home gardens and used in traditional medicine. In Japan, the shiso leaf is an integral part of cuisine, symbolizing good luck and happiness.

Production

Perilla is cultivated in various parts of Asia, including Korea, Japan, India, and China, as well as in gardens worldwide for its ornamental and culinary value. It thrives in well-drained soil in full sun to partial shade and is harvested for its leaves and seeds.

Other Facts

Perilla oil, extracted from the seeds, is rich in omega-3 fatty acids, making it a valuable nutritional supplement.

Peruvian pepper

Peruvian Pepper, known scientifically as Schinus molle, is a distinctive spice native to the Peruvian Andes but now found in various parts of the world. Also known as the Peruvian peppertree, it belongs to the Anacardiaceae family, which includes cashews and mangos. It is characterized by its slender, weeping form, with narrow, lance-shaped leaves and clusters of small, pinkish-red berries.

Culinary Uses

The dried berries of the Peruvian Pepper are used as a spice, offering a mildly spicy and sweet flavor with hints of citrus. They are often used whole or ground in Peruvian and South American cuisines to season meats, sauces, and traditional dishes. The unique flavor profile of Peruvian Pepper makes it a versatile spice, suitable for culinary experimentation in a variety of global dishes. It pairs well with ingredients like tomatoes, garlic, and herbs, adding a complex layer of flavor to soups, stews, and marinades.

Medicinal Properties

Traditionally, Peruvian Pepper has been used in herbal medicine for its anti-inflammatory, antiseptic, and analgesic properties. The berries and leaves of the plant are believed to help relieve rheumatic pain and respiratory conditions. However, it's important to use Peruvian Pepper with caution, as it belongs to a family known for allergenic compounds.

Cultural Significance

In its native Andes and throughout South America, Peruvian Pepper holds cultural significance for its decorative beauty, culinary uses, and traditional medicinal applications. The tree is often planted in public spaces and gardens for its attractive appearance and shade-providing canopy.

Production

Schinus molle thrives in warm, dry climates and is now cultivated in various parts of the world, including California, the Mediterranean, and parts of Africa and Australia, for its ornamental value and spice production. The berries are harvested when ripe, dried, and then can be used whole or ground.

Other Facts

Peruvian Pepper is not related to black or white pepper (Piper nigrum) but offers a distinct flavor that can complement or substitute for traditional pepper in recipes.

Pipicha

Pipicha, also known as Porophyllum tagetoides, is a lesser-known herb indigenous to Mexico and Central America. It belongs to the Asteraceae family and is characterized by its long, slender leaves and aromatic properties, distinct from those of more familiar herbs like basil. Pipicha has a unique flavor profile, often described as a combination of citrus, cilantro, and arugula, with a hint of mint and lemon.

Culinary Uses

Pipicha is utilized in traditional Mexican cuisine, particularly in the southern states. Its robust flavor is well-suited to salsas, soups, salads, and dishes featuring corn, beans, and fish. The herb is often used fresh, added towards the end of cooking to preserve its delicate aroma and taste. Pipicha is also a key ingredient in green moles and can be used as a garnish for various dishes, imparting a refreshing, herbal note.

Medicinal Properties

While not as widely recognized for its medicinal properties as some herbs, pipicha is believed to have digestive benefits in traditional Mexican herbal medicine.

Cultural Significance

In its native regions, pipicha is more than just a culinary herb; it represents a connection to traditional farming practices and cuisine. It is valued for its unique flavor and is often grown in home gardens and small-scale agricultural settings, reflecting the rich biodiversity of Mexican flora.

Production

Pipicha is primarily cultivated in Mexico and Central America, where it thrives in warm, sunny environments. The herb is typically harvested by hand, ensuring the leaves are fresh and aromatic at the time of use. Although not as widely available as more common herbs, pipicha is gaining recognition among chefs and food enthusiasts interested in exploring traditional Mexican ingredients.

Other Facts

Due to its distinctive taste, pipicha is not a direct substitute for any single herb but can be used to add complexity and depth to dishes. For those looking to experiment with pipicha, it is best sourced from specialty markets or grown from seeds in a home garden.

Poppy seed

Poppy seed, derived from the opium poppy (Papaver somniferum), is a widely used spice in global cuisines, celebrated for its nutty flavor and crunchy texture. This small, slate-blue seed belongs to the family Papaveraceae and has been cultivated for thousands of years, not only for culinary uses but also for its medicinal properties. The plant is characterized by its beautiful flowers, which can range in color from white to purple, and its round seed pods from which the seeds are harvested.

Culinary Uses

Poppy seeds are a versatile ingredient used in a variety of dishes, including bread, pastries, and desserts, as well as savory dishes. They are a key component in lemon poppy seed cakes, muffins, and bagels, and are used to thicken sauces and fillings. In Eastern European cuisine, poppy seeds are ground and mixed with sweeteners to make a paste used in pastries like strudel and kolaches. They also add texture and flavor to salad dressings, noodles, and vegetable dishes.

Medicinal Properties

Traditionally, poppy seeds have been used for their nutritional benefits, as they are rich in linoleic acid, oleic acid, and dietary fiber. While poppy seeds themselves do not contain narcotic properties, the plant they come from is known for producing opium alkaloids used in medicine for pain relief.

Cultural Significance

Poppy seeds hold significant cultural importance in various traditions, symbolizing sleep and peace due to the sedative effects of the opium poppy. They are used in rituals and dishes that mark important life events and holidays, reflecting their significance in culinary and cultural practices.

Production

The primary producers of poppy seeds include countries in Central and Eastern Europe, such as the Czech Republic, Hungary, and Poland, as well as Turkey and India. The cultivation of poppy for seed production requires specific climatic conditions, and the seeds are harvested after the flower petals fall and the seed pods dry.

Other Facts

While consuming foods with poppy seeds in normal culinary amounts is generally safe, they can contain trace amounts of opium alkaloids, which may affect drug testing results.

Purslane

Purslane, scientifically known as Portulaca oleracea, is a resilient herb commonly regarded as a weed in many gardens but celebrated in various cuisines worldwide for its unique flavor and nutritional benefits. This succulent annual plant is part of the Portulacaceae family and thrives in a variety of climates, often found in garden cracks and arid environments. Purslane has fleshy, green leaves and small yellow flowers, making it easily identifiable. It is native to the Middle Eastern regions but has spread globally to become a ubiquitous plant.

Culinary Uses

Purslane's leaves and stems offer a slightly sour and salty flavor, reminiscent of spinach and watercress. It is a versatile ingredient used in salads, soups, stews, and sandwiches. In Mediterranean cuisine, purslane is often added to salads and yogurt dishes for its tangy taste. It pairs well with cucumbers, tomatoes, and citrus dressings. Purslane can also be cooked, serving as a great addition to stir-fries and egg dishes, where its slight mucilaginous quality can be beneficial.

Medicinal Properties

Purslane is highly regarded for its health benefits, containing more Omega-3 fatty acids than any other leafy vegetable plant. It is also rich in vitamins A, C, and E, which are potent antioxidants, as well as magnesium, calcium, potassium, and iron. Traditionally, purslane has been used to treat various ailments, including digestive issues and skin conditions. Its high Omega-3 content makes it beneficial for cardiovascular health and anti-inflammatory purposes.

Cultural Significance

In many cultures, purslane is more than just a culinary herb; it is a symbol of resilience and life. It has been consumed for centuries, with its use dating back to ancient Egyptian and Greek societies. In some regions, it is considered a symbol of good luck.

Production

Purslane is a plant that requires little water and can grow in poor soil conditions, making it an eco-friendly crop. It is cultivated in many parts of the world, particularly in Europe, Asia, and the Mediterranean regions, for both its culinary uses and health benefits. The plant is harvested for its leaves and stems, which are best when picked young for their tenderness and flavor.

Quassia

Quassia, known for its bitter properties, is a remarkable herb used in various cultural and medicinal contexts around the world. Quassia refers to plants within the genus Quassia, with Quassia amara being one of the most notable species. This genus is part of the Simaroubaceae family, native to the tropical regions of the Americas, particularly in the Caribbean and parts of South America. Quassia amara is a small tree or shrub, recognized by its compound leaves, red to pink flowers, and the production of a deep red wood that is the source of its potent bitterness.

Culinary Uses

Quassia's intense bitterness has found its way into the culinary world, primarily as a flavoring agent in foods, beverages, and notably in bitters and aperitifs. The wood and bark of Quassia amara are used to make a bitter extract, which is then incorporated into these drinks to impart a distinctive flavor. While not widely used in everyday cooking due to its strong taste, Quassia is appreciated in small quantities for its ability to stimulate digestion and enhance the flavors of certain dishes and drinks.

Medicinal Properties

Quassia amara boasts a variety of medicinal uses, primarily attributed to its bitter compounds, including quassin, one of the most bitter substances known. These compounds have been used traditionally to stimulate appetite, improve digestion, and treat conditions such as malaria, fevers, and intestinal parasites. Quassia also possesses anti-inflammatory and antiviral properties, making it a valuable herb in traditional medicine practices.

Cultural Significance

In the regions where Quassia amara is native, it holds significant cultural value, often used in traditional medicine and ceremonies. Its name originates from a West Indian slave, Quassi, who used the plant for medicinal purposes, highlighting its deep-rooted history in folk medicine.

Production

Quassia amara is cultivated in tropical climates, with a focus on sustainable harvesting practices due to the plant's medicinal value. The wood and bark are the primary parts used for their bitter principles. It is harvested, dried, and then either sold in bulk or processed into extracts or powders for medicinal and culinary uses.

Red rice powder

Red rice powder, derived from unpolished red rice, is a nutritious and colorful ingredient used in various culinary traditions around the world. Unlike white rice, red rice gets its unique color from an outer layer that contains anthocyanins, which are beneficial antioxidants. This type of rice is grown in different parts of the world, including Southeast Asia and parts of the Himalayas, where it is a staple in the local diet. Red rice is valued not only for its nutritional profile but also for its nutty flavor and slightly chewy texture.

Culinary Uses

Red rice powder is made by grinding dried red rice into a fine powder. It can be used in a variety of dishes, adding a distinct color and a mildly nutty flavor. In Asian cuisine, red rice powder is often used to make traditional sweets, bread, pancakes, and even as a thickening agent for sauces and soups. Its rich color also makes it a popular choice for naturally coloring foods. Beyond its use in traditional dishes, red rice powder is also incorporated into modern recipes for health-conscious consumers, including smoothies, protein bars, and gluten-free baked goods.

Medicinal Properties

Red rice, and by extension red rice powder, is known for its potential health benefits. It is rich in fiber, which aids in digestion and can help in managing blood sugar levels. The presence of antioxidants like anthocyanins contributes to heart health and may reduce the risk of chronic diseases. Additionally, red rice contains vitamins and minerals such as magnesium, iron, and zinc.

Cultural Significance

In the regions where it is cultivated, red rice holds cultural importance, often associated with prosperity and health. It is sometimes used in ceremonial dishes and special occasions, reflecting its value beyond everyday nutrition.

Production

The cultivation of red rice is similar to other rice varieties, but it often requires specific climatic conditions to thrive. After harvest, the rice is dried and then ground into powder. This process preserves the nutrients and flavor of the red rice, making the powder a versatile and healthful ingredient. The production of red rice powder is most common in countries where red rice is a traditional crop, including Thailand, Bhutan, and parts of India.

Rice paddy herb

Red Rice Paddy Herb, scientifically known as Limnophila aromatica, is a distinctive herb native to Southeast Asia, flourishing in the aquatic environments of rice paddies and shallow waters. Unlike the land-grown herbs like basil, Red Rice Paddy Herb thrives in wet conditions, contributing to its unique characteristics and uses in culinary practices. This herb belongs to the Plantaginaceae family and is notable for its narrow, pointed leaves that range in color from green to a deep reddish-purple, depending on the variety and growing conditions.

Culinary Uses

Red Rice Paddy Herb is cherished for its unique flavor profile, offering a combination of citrus and cumin-like taste, which adds a complex flavor dimension to dishes. It is a staple in Vietnamese cuisine, most famously used in sour soup dishes like Canh Chua, where its distinctive aroma and taste are integral to the soup's flavor. The herb is also used in salads, fish dishes, and other Southeast Asian recipes, where its fresh, citrusy notes can truly shine. Its ability to withstand long cooking times makes it a versatile herb in the culinary world, enhancing the dishes with its intense aroma and flavor.

Medicinal Properties

Traditionally, Red Rice Paddy Herb has been utilized in folk medicine for its health benefits. While it is not as extensively studied as some other herbs, it is believed to possess anti-inflammatory and antimicrobial properties, contributing to its use in treating ailments and promoting overall health in the regions where it is native.

Cultural Significance

In Southeast Asia, Red Rice Paddy Herb is more than just a culinary ingredient; it is a part of the agricultural landscape and culture, especially in Vietnam. Its presence in rice paddies symbolizes the symbiotic relationship between agriculture and local ecosystems, showcasing the importance of biodiversity in traditional farming practices.

Production

The cultivation of Red Rice Paddy Herb is closely tied to the rice-growing regions of Southeast Asia, where it naturally occurs in the wet, humid conditions ideal for its growth. Harvesting involves collecting the tender tops and leaves of the plant, which are then used fresh to preserve their aromatic properties. Due to its specific growing conditions, it is less commonly found in markets outside of Southeast Asia but is sometimes available in Asian specialty stores.

Rosemary

Rosemary, renowned for its fragrant and needle-like leaves, is a perennial herb that plays a vital role in a variety of cuisines across the globe, especially in Mediterranean dishes. Rosemary (Rosmarinus officinalis) is a member of the mint family, Lamiaceae, and originates from the Mediterranean region. This herb is characterized by its woody stems and evergreen leaves that are rich in aromatic oils. Rosemary's versatility is evident in its ability to thrive in both kitchen gardens and wild landscapes.

Culinary Uses

Rosemary's flavor is unmistakably aromatic, with a pine-like fragrance and a slightly bitter, astringent taste. It is a fundamental herb in Mediterranean cuisine, used to season meats, soups, and stews, as well as vegetables and sauces. Rosemary is particularly well-suited to flavoring lamb, chicken, and pork, and it pairs beautifully with garlic, lemon, and olive oil. Its robust nature allows it to withstand long cooking times, making it ideal for roasting and grilling. Fresh or dried, rosemary enhances dishes with its distinctive flavor and is often used in marinades and as a garnish.

Medicinal Properties

Historically, rosemary has been valued for its medicinal properties, including its ability to improve memory, relieve muscle pain and spasm, stimulate the immune and circulatory systems, and promote hair growth. It is rich in antioxidants and anti-inflammatory compounds, which can help neutralize harmful free radicals in the body.

Cultural Significance

In many cultures, rosemary symbolizes remembrance, love, and loyalty, and it is often used in wedding ceremonies, funerals, and other significant rituals. It has a long history of use in both culinary and medicinal contexts, dating back to ancient civilizations, including the Greeks, Romans, and Egyptians.

Production

The production of rosemary is widespread, with countries in the Mediterranean region, such as Spain, Italy, and France, being major producers. It is cultivated worldwide in climates that can support its growth, including parts of the Americas and Africa. Rosemary is harvested for its leaves, which are used both fresh and dried, and for its essential oil, which is extracted and used in various products.

Rue

Rue, known scientifically as Ruta graveolens, is a perennial herb native to the Balkan Peninsula, now widespread across the world, particularly in Mediterranean regions. Belonging to the Rutaceae family, rue is characterized by its strong, pungent aroma and bitter taste. The plant features bluish-green leaves and during summer, it blooms with small yellow flowers. Traditionally, rue has been cultivated not only for its culinary and medicinal properties but also for its symbolic significance in various cultures.

Culinary Uses

In the culinary world, rue's potent flavor and bitterness mean it is used sparingly. It is an ingredient in certain traditional dishes in Mediterranean cuisines, such as the Italian grappa herb-flavored spirit and various meat dishes, offering a unique, somewhat citrusy flavor profile. Due to its strong taste, it is recommended to use rue in moderation, as it can dominate other flavors in a dish.

Medicinal Properties

Historically, rue has been valued for its range of medicinal properties. It was used in ancient times as a remedy for various ailments, including digestive issues, nervous system disorders, and as an antispasmodic. Rue contains compounds such as flavonoids and alkaloids, which contribute to its therapeutic effects. However, it is important to note that rue should be used with caution medicinally, as it can be toxic in high doses and may cause skin irritation or photosensitivity.

Cultural Significance

Rue holds a significant place in many cultural traditions, symbolizing repentance, remembrance, and protection. In ancient Rome, it was considered a powerful protective herb against evil spirits and was used in various rituals. It has also been used in traditional folk practices to ward off curses and evil eyes.

Production

Rue thrives in hot, dry climates and is commonly found in herb gardens and wild in its native and naturalized regions. It is cultivated for its leaves, which are harvested before the plant flowers for culinary and medicinal uses. The plant is drought-tolerant and requires little maintenance, making it a resilient herb for cultivation.

Safflower

Safflower, known for its bright yellow and orange flowers, is a highly valued crop used for its seeds and oil, rather than as a traditional herb or spice. Safflower (Carthamus tinctorius) belongs to the Asteraceae family, similar to sunflowers, and is native to arid environments in the Middle East and India. It is an annual plant, characterized by its tall stalks, spiny leaves, and vibrant flowers. Historically, safflower was cultivated for its flowers, used in coloring and flavoring foods, and in textiles dyes.

Culinary Uses

While not commonly used as a herb or spice in cooking, safflower oil, extracted from the seeds of the plant, is widely used in cooking and salad dressings due to its neutral flavor and high smoke point. The oil is prized for its nutritional benefits, being rich in unsaturated fatty acids. The petals of the safflower plant have been used historically as a cheaper substitute for saffron, providing a similar coloring to dishes, though with a milder flavor.

Medicinal Properties

Safflower has been used in traditional medicine for various purposes. The oil is known for its health benefits, including improving cholesterol levels, reducing inflammation, and promoting skin health. Additionally, safflower tea, made from the petals of the plant, is believed to have antioxidant properties and has been used to treat fevers and as a laxative.

Cultural Significance

Safflower has a long history of cultivation dating back to ancient Egypt, where it was used for its oil and as a coloring agent for clothing and cosmetics. In traditional Chinese medicine, safflower is used to stimulate blood circulation and alleviate pain, particularly menstrual pain.

Production

The main producers of safflower include India, the United States, and Mexico. The plant is cultivated in arid and semi-arid regions, with seeds harvested for their oil. Safflower oil is extracted through cold pressing or chemical extraction methods.

Other Facts

Safflower is also used in the paint industry as a drying oil and in the cosmetics industry for its moisturizing properties. The plant is beneficial for soil health and is sometimes used in crop rotation to improve soil conditions.

Saffron

Saffron, celebrated for its vivid crimson strands, is not only the world's most expensive spice by weight but also a highly esteemed ingredient in culinary traditions across the globe. Saffron is derived from the flower of Crocus sativus, a member of the Iridaceae family, and is native to Southwest Asia, with cultivation extending to the Mediterranean, Middle East, and South Asia. The spice consists of the flower's dried stigmas, which are laboriously hand-harvested, contributing to its high cost. Each flower produces only three stigmas, requiring thousands of flowers to yield a single pound of saffron.

Culinary Uses

Saffron's flavor is subtly earthy, with a complex aroma and a slightly sweet, floral taste. It is famed for imparting a luminous yellow-orange hue to dishes. Saffron is indispensable in many international cuisines, prominently featuring in Spanish paella, Italian risotto Milanese, French bouillabaisse, and Persian rice dishes. It is also used in sweets and pastries for its color and aroma. Due to its intense flavor, saffron is used sparingly, with just a few strands sufficing to flavor and color an entire dish.

Medicinal Properties

Historically, saffron has been used for its medicinal properties, including as an antidepressant, anti-inflammatory, and antispasmodic agent. It is rich in antioxidants, which may contribute to health benefits such as improved mood, increased libido, and enhanced overall well-being. Research suggests that saffron may have protective effects against certain diseases, though its high cost can limit its use in medicinal contexts.

Cultural Significance

Saffron holds a place of honor in many cultures, symbolizing light, happiness, and wealth. It has been used in religious ceremonies, as a dye for royal garments, and in traditional medicine for millennia. The spice's value and the labor-intensive process of harvesting have made it a symbol of luxury and dedication.

Production

Iran is the world's largest producer of saffron, contributing the majority of the global supply, followed by countries like Spain, India, and Greece. The cultivation of saffron is highly labor-intensive, as the stigmas must be handpicked from the flowers at dawn before being carefully dried. This meticulous process justifies the spice's hefty price tag.

Sage

Sage, renowned for its aromatic leaves, is a staple herb in various cuisines, particularly in European dishes. Sage (Salvia officinalis) belongs to the mint family, Lamiaceae, and is native to the Mediterranean region. It is a perennial plant, characterized by its woody stems, grayish leaves, and purplish flowers. The herb is known for its earthy and slightly peppery flavor, with hints of mint, eucalyptus, and lemon.

Culinary Uses

Sage's robust flavor profile makes it a key ingredient in European cuisine, notably in Italian, British, and French dishes. It pairs well with poultry, pork, and beef, and is essential in the preparation of sausages, stuffings, and sauces. Sage is also used to flavor butter, cheese, and vegetable dishes. Its leaves can be used fresh or dried, although fresh sage offers a milder taste. When cooking with sage, it is typically added at the beginning of the cooking process to allow its flavors to infuse the dish.

Medicinal Properties

Traditionally, sage has been valued for its medicinal properties, including its ability to aid digestion, relieve sore throats, and boost memory and cognitive functions. Sage contains various essential oils, flavonoids, and phenolic acids, which contribute to its antioxidant, anti-inflammatory, and antimicrobial properties.

Cultural Significance

Sage holds a place of esteem in many cultures for its culinary, medicinal, and spiritual uses. In ancient times, it was celebrated for its healing properties and was often used in rituals and ceremonies for purification and protection.

Production

Sage is cultivated worldwide, thriving in well-drained soil under full sun. It is harvested for its leaves, which are used both fresh and dried for culinary and medicinal purposes. The plant can be easily grown in herb gardens, containers, and even indoors, making it accessible to home cooks and herbalists alike.

Other Facts

In addition to its use in cooking and traditional medicine, sage essential oil is used in aromatherapy and natural cosmetic products for its calming and cleansing properties..

Salad burnet

Salad Burnet, recognized for its light, cucumber-like flavor, is a perennial herb that enriches a variety of dishes with its fresh, green leaves. Salad Burnet (Sanguisorba minor) belongs to the rose family, Rosaceae, and is native to Europe, but has been naturalized in many parts of North America. It is characterized by its small, serrated leaves and round, reddish flower heads that bloom in early summer.

Culinary Uses

Salad Burnet's flavor is reminiscent of cucumber, making it a delightful addition to salads, dips, and cold beverages. It is used to impart a fresh, cucumbery taste to cream cheeses, vinegars, and dressings. The herb can also be chopped and sprinkled over soups, stews, and grilled meats as a garnish. Due to its mild flavor, Salad Burnet is best used fresh; the leaves lose much of their taste when dried.

Medicinal Properties

Traditionally, Salad Burnet has been utilized for its astringent and healing properties. It has been used to treat wounds and skin conditions due to its ability to reduce bleeding and promote healing. The herb is also known for its diuretic effects and has been used in herbal medicine to aid digestion and improve liver function.

Cultural Significance

While not as culturally significant as some other herbs, Salad Burnet has been used in European herbalism since the Middle Ages for both its culinary and medicinal qualities. It was popular in Tudor England as a salad ingredient and has been a traditional component of English cottage gardens.

Production

Salad Burnet is easy to grow in temperate climates, preferring sunny locations and well-drained soil. It is a hardy herb that can tolerate drought and is often found in meadows and grasslands. The plant forms a low-growing rosette of leaves that can be harvested throughout the growing season, providing a continuous supply of fresh leaves.

Other Facts

Salad Burnet is valued in landscaping for its attractive foliage and flowers. The plant is drought-tolerant and can be used in xeriscaping and as an ornamental border.

Sassafras

Sassafras, known for its distinctive aroma and flavor, has been a notable ingredient in various culinary and medicinal traditions, particularly in North America. Sassafras (Sassafras albidum) is a deciduous tree native to eastern North America, belonging to the family Lauraceae. It is easily recognizable by its unique leaf shapes, which can vary even on the same tree, and by its aromatic properties, especially in the root and bark.

Culinary Uses

Historically, sassafras played a key role in culinary applications, most famously as the original flavoring of root beer. The root and bark were used to make tea, and the leaves, when dried and ground, become filé powder, an essential ingredient in Cajun and Creole cuisines, particularly in gumbo. Sassafras imparts a distinct flavor that is a mix of sweet, spicy, and lemony notes.

Medicinal Properties

Traditionally, sassafras has been used for a variety of medicinal purposes, including as a diuretic, stimulant, and treatment for skin diseases and rheumatism. It was believed to purify blood and was used in tonics. However, the FDA banned the use of sassafras oil and safrole, one of its constituents, in commercially mass-produced foods and drugs due to carcinogenic properties found in animal studies.

Cultural Significance

Sassafras holds a special place in the cultural heritage of many Native American tribes and early American settlers. It was used in traditional ceremonies, as a health remedy, and even as a building material due to its aromatic properties believed to repel insects and disease.

Production

Sassafras trees grow widely in the eastern United States, from Maine to Florida and west to Texas and Kansas. While not cultivated on a large scale like other crops, the tree is harvested from the wild for personal use and small-scale commercial purposes. The roots, bark, and leaves are the most commonly used parts of the plant.

Other Facts

The use of sassafras in foods and beverages is now regulated due to health concerns related to safrole.

Sesame Seed

Sesame seeds, known for their nutty taste and delicate crunch, are widely used across various cuisines around the world. Originating from the sesame plant (Sesamum indicum), which belongs to the Pedaliaceae family, these tiny seeds have been cultivated since ancient times. Native to Africa and parts of India, sesame seeds are one of the oldest oilseed crops known, with a rich history of both culinary and medicinal use.

Culinary Uses

Sesame seeds are incredibly versatile in the kitchen. They are a key ingredient in Middle Eastern tahini (sesame paste) and the sweet confection known as halva. Sesame oil, extracted from the seeds, is a staple in Asian cooking, prized for its high smoke point and rich flavor. The seeds themselves are often toasted and sprinkled over salads, breads, sushi, and desserts for added texture and taste. Black sesame seeds, in particular, are used for their visual contrast and slightly stronger flavor.

Medicinal Properties

They are rich in essential nutrients, including calcium, magnesium, zinc, fiber, iron, B vitamins, and antioxidants. Sesame oil is known for its anti-inflammatory properties, and the seeds are believed to support heart health, reduce cholesterol levels, and aid in digestion.

Cultural Significance

Sesame seeds symbolize immortality in Hindu traditions and are used in rituals and ceremonies. In Middle Eastern cultures, sesame seeds are a symbol of blessing and prosperity.

Production

The leading producers of sesame seeds include Tanzania, Myanmar, India, and Sudan. The plant prefers warm climates and well-drained soil, making it suitable for cultivation in various parts of the world. Sesame seeds are harvested from the pods of the sesame plant, which burst open when they reach maturity, a characteristic referred to as dehiscence.

Other Facts

Sesame seeds are available in several forms, including hulled, unhulled, toasted, and as oil. Each form offers different flavors and nutritional benefits. For example, hulled sesame seeds have a milder taste and are more common in Western cuisines, while unhulled seeds are more nutrient-dense.

Savory, summer

Summer Savory, known for its peppery and slightly spicy flavor, is a beloved herb in many culinary traditions around the world, especially in European cuisines. Summer Savory (Satureja hortensis) belongs to the mint family, Lamiaceae, and is native to warm temperate regions of Southern Europe and the Mediterranean. It is an annual herb, characterized by its fine, green leaves and branching stems, blooming with small, lavender-pink flowers in late summer.

Culinary Uses

Summer Savory's flavor is pungent and peppery, with notes of marjoram, thyme, and mint, making it a versatile herb in the kitchen. It is traditionally used in bean dishes, soups, stews, and with meats, particularly pork and poultry. The herb pairs well with vegetables, eggs, and cheeses, and is a key ingredient in the classic herb blend Herbes de Provence. It is also used to season sausages and stuffings, adding depth and warmth to dishes. Summer Savory is best used fresh but can also be dried to preserve its flavor for out-of-season use.

Medicinal Properties

Traditionally, Summer Savory has been used for its digestive and antiseptic properties. It is believed to aid in digestion and relieve symptoms of gastrointestinal discomfort. The herb contains compounds that have been shown to have antimicrobial and antioxidant effects, contributing to its health benefits.

Cultural Significance

In culinary history, Summer Savory has been appreciated for centuries for its seasoning capabilities and medicinal uses. It was known to the Romans and has been cultivated in kitchen gardens throughout Europe since the Middle Ages. The herb's name itself suggests its application in enhancing the flavors of summer dishes.

Production

Summer Savory is cultivated in gardens and farms in temperate climates worldwide. It thrives in well-drained soil and full sun, making it a suitable herb for both commercial and home gardening. The leaves are harvested before the plant flowers for optimal flavor and can be used fresh, frozen, or dried.

Savory, winter

Winter Savory, with its robust and peppery flavor, is an essential herb in various culinary traditions, particularly favored in European cuisine. Winter Savory (Satureja montana) belongs to the mint family, Lamiaceae, and is native to warm temperate regions of Europe and the Mediterranean. Unlike its annual counterpart, Summer Savory, Winter Savory is a perennial plant, characterized by its woody stems, leathery leaves, and small white or pink flowers.

Culinary Uses

Winter Savory's flavor is more pungent and bitter compared to Summer Savory, with a complex profile that hints at thyme and mint. It is widely used in dishes that require a bold herbaceous note, such as bean stews, meats, and hearty vegetable dishes. The herb pairs excellently with mushrooms, lentils, and poultry. It is also a component of the traditional herb blend Herbes de Provence and is used to season sausages, stuffings, and sauces. Due to its strong flavor, Winter Savory should be used sparingly and can be added both at the beginning or end of cooking to adjust the intensity of its taste.

Medicinal Properties

Historically, Winter Savory has been utilized for its antiseptic, digestive, and anti-inflammatory properties. It is believed to aid digestion, relieve symptoms of gastrointestinal discomfort, and has been used in traditional remedies for coughs and throat infections. The herb contains thymol and carvacrol, compounds known for their antimicrobial and antioxidant effects.

Cultural Significance

In traditional European herbalism, Winter Savory has been valued for both its culinary and medicinal qualities. It has been cultivated in herb gardens for centuries and is known for its ability to endure colder climates, providing a source of fresh flavor throughout the winter months.

Production

Winter Savory is grown in herb gardens and farms in regions with temperate climates. It prefers full sun and well-drained soil, making it suitable for cultivation in many parts of the world. The leaves are harvested as needed for culinary use and can be used fresh, dried, or frozen to preserve their flavor.

Shiso

Shiso, also known as perilla, is a distinctive herb integral to Japanese, Korean, and Southeast Asian cuisines. Shiso (Perilla frutescens) belongs to the mint family, Lamiaceae, and is known for its broad, textured leaves, which come in both green and purple varieties. This annual herb is celebrated for its unique flavor profile, which can be described as a combination of mint, basil, cilantro, and a hint of cinnamon or anise.

Culinary Uses

Shiso's flavor is both refreshing and complex, making it a versatile ingredient in a wide range of dishes. In Japanese cuisine, green shiso leaves are often used as a garnish for sushi and sashimi, mixed into salads, or incorporated into pickles. Purple shiso, on the other hand, is commonly used to color and flavor umeboshi (pickled plums) and to add depth to rice dishes. Korean cuisine utilizes perilla leaves in salads, grilled meats, and as a wrapping leaf, while its seeds are used to produce a flavorful oil. Shiso can also be found in cocktails and desserts for an aromatic twist.

Medicinal Properties

Traditionally, shiso has been used in Asian herbal medicine for its potential health benefits, including anti-inflammatory, antipyretic (fever-reducing), and antiseptic properties. It is believed to help relieve symptoms of asthma, colds, and other respiratory ailments. Shiso is also rich in antioxidants and contains rosmarinic acid, which may contribute to its anti-allergic effects.

Cultural Significance

In addition to its culinary uses, shiso holds cultural importance in Japan and other Asian countries, where it is often used in ceremonies and as a decorative plant. The herb's vibrant leaves are symbolic of cleanliness and have been used traditionally to preserve and purify food.

Production

Shiso is cultivated in gardens and farms across Japan, Korea, China, and other parts of Southeast Asia, thriving in sunny, well-drained conditions. It can also be grown in temperate climates around the world, including in home gardens.

Other Facts

Shiso leaves can be used fresh, dried, or pickled, offering a range of flavors depending on the preparation.

Sichuan pepper

Sichuan pepper, known for its unique aroma and numbing sensation, plays a central role in Chinese cuisine, particularly in Sichuan dishes. Sichuan pepper (Zanthoxylum simulans) is not a true pepper but a spice derived from the husks of the seeds of several species of the genus Zanthoxylum, which belongs to the rue or citrus family, Rutaceae. Unlike black or white pepper, Sichuan pepper imparts a characteristic tingling sensation on the palate, along with a complex flavor profile that includes hints of lemon and spice.

Culinary Uses

Sichuan pepper's distinctive taste is essential in many Chinese dishes, such as mapo tofu, Sichuan hot pots, and kung pao chicken. It is one of the components of the famous Chinese five-spice powder, along with star anise, cloves, Chinese cinnamon, and fennel seeds. The spice is used both whole and ground, often toasted to enhance its flavor. Sichuan pepper pairs well with meats, poultry, and in spicy sauces, contributing both aroma and a numbing effect that is characteristic of Sichuan cuisine.

Medicinal Properties

Traditionally, Sichuan pepper has been used in Chinese medicine for its potential health benefits, including stimulating circulation, reducing pain, and for its antimicrobial properties. The numbing effect of Sichuan pepper is attributed to hydroxy-alpha sanshool, a compound that can affect the sensory nerves.

Cultural Significance

Sichuan pepper holds a significant place in Chinese culinary culture, symbolizing the bold and complex flavors of Sichuan cuisine. It is also used in Tibetan, Bhutanese, Nepali, and Japanese cuisines, showcasing its broad cultural impact beyond China.

Production

Sichuan pepper is primarily produced in the Sichuan province of China, but it is also harvested in other regions of China and the Himalayas. The spice is derived from the outer husk of the fruit, which is dried and then either used whole or ground into powder.

Other Facts

Despite its name, Sichuan pepper was banned from import into the United States until 2005 due to concerns over a citrus canker; however, it is now available, provided it is heat-treated to kill the bacteria.

Silphium

Silphium, a now-extinct herb, was once a highly prized plant in the ancient Mediterranean world, particularly by the Greeks and Romans. It belonged to the genus Ferula, related to the fennel and giant fennel plants. Silphium was noted for its thick stalk, broad leaves, and small yellow flowers. Its exact flavor profile and appearance are largely speculative, derived from historical texts, as no samples of the plant exist today. It was said to have a taste that combined elements of garlic, onion, and other strong savory flavors.

Culinary Uses

Silphium was widely used in ancient cooking, both as a seasoning and as a key ingredient in various dishes. It was reputed to enhance the flavor of a wide range of foods, from meats to vegetables and was also used in pickling. The plant's resin, known as laser or lasarpicium, was particularly valued for its strong, unique taste.

Medicinal Properties

The herb was renowned for its medicinal properties, with applications ranging from general health and well-being to specific treatments for coughs, digestive issues, and as a contraceptive, according to some historical sources.

Cultural Significance

Silphium held immense cultural and economic significance in the ancient world, especially for the city of Cyrene in North Africa. It became a symbol of the city's wealth and was even depicted on Cyrenian coins. The rarity and importance of silphium contributed to its legendary status in history.

Production

Silphium was native to a narrow coastal strip in the Cyrenaica region of Libya. It is believed that the plant was never successfully cultivated and was harvested from the wild until it became extinct, possibly due to overharvesting, climate change, or overgrazing by livestock. The last recorded reference to silphium was in the 4th century AD, after which it disappeared from historical records.

Other Facts

The mystery surrounding silphium, including its exact identity, uses, and sudden disappearance, continues to fascinate historians, botanists, and gastronomes. Its loss is often cited as one of the first recorded instances of overexploitation of a natural resource leading to extinction..

Sorrel

Sorrel, characterized by its tangy, lemony flavor, is a perennial herb that enriches a variety of dishes across many cuisines, especially in Europe. Sorrel (Rumex acetosa) belongs to the Polygonaceae family and is known for its bright green, lance-shaped leaves. It thrives in temperate regions and is valued both for its culinary versatility and medicinal properties.

Culinary Uses

The sharp, acidic taste of sorrel makes it a popular ingredient in salads, soups, sauces, and egg dishes. It's particularly famous for its role in classic French cuisine, such as in the soup "soupe aux herbes" and the sauce for "poached salmon." Eastern European cuisines often use sorrel in borscht and other hearty soups, taking advantage of its vibrant flavor to add depth to dishes. Sorrel can be eaten raw or cooked, though its acidity mellows with cooking. Due to its strong flavor, it is often used in moderation and pairs well with fish, chicken, and potatoes.

Medicinal Properties

Traditionally, sorrel has been used for its health benefits, including vitamin C and A content, aiding in digestion and promoting skin health. However, due to its high oxalic acid content, consumption should be moderate, especially for individuals with certain health conditions, such as kidney stones.

Cultural Significance

Sorrel has been cultivated and used in food and medicine for centuries, dating back to ancient Egypt. It holds a place in traditional medicine in many cultures for its purported health benefits and is celebrated in various European cuisines for its unique flavor.

Production

Sorrel is grown in herb gardens and farms in temperate climates worldwide. It is harvested for its leaves, which are best when young and tender. The herb can be grown from seed or division and prefers well-drained soil and partial to full sun. Sorrel is a hardy plant, often one of the first to appear in the spring garden.

Other Facts

There are several varieties of sorrel, including garden sorrel (Rumex acetosa) and French sorrel (Rumex scutatus), each with a slightly different flavor profile.

Spearmint

Spearmint, with its refreshing and mildly sweet flavor, is a popular herb in various cuisines around the world. Spearmint (Mentha spicata) belongs to the mint family, Lamiaceae, and is native to Europe and Asia. It is a perennial herb, characterized by its bright green, pointed leaves, and distinctive minty aroma. Spearmint is more subtle in flavor compared to its relative, peppermint, making it a versatile addition to both savory and sweet dishes.

Culinary Uses

Spearmint's mild, sweet flavor makes it a favorite in a wide array of dishes and beverages. It is commonly used in Middle Eastern cuisine, featuring in salads like tabbouleh, in yogurt dressings, and in meat dishes. Spearmint is also a key ingredient in mint sauce, a classic accompaniment to lamb. In beverages, it is used to flavor teas, cocktails such as the mojito, and non-alcoholic drinks like lemonade. Fresh spearmint leaves are often used as a garnish or chopped and added to desserts for a burst of freshness.

Medicinal Properties

Traditionally, spearmint has been valued for its digestive benefits, helping to relieve symptoms of indigestion, nausea, and gas. It is also known for its soothing properties, aiding in the reduction of headaches and stress. Spearmint tea is a common home remedy for soothing sore throats and improving oral health due to its antimicrobial properties.

Cultural Significance

Spearmint has been used for centuries in folk medicine and culinary traditions around the globe. Its refreshing aroma and taste have made it a symbol of hospitality in many cultures, often served to guests in the form of tea or used to flavor dishes and refreshments.

Production

Spearmint is cultivated worldwide, thriving in temperate climates. It is harvested for its leaves, which are used fresh, dried, or distilled to extract spearmint oil. The herb can easily be grown in gardens and containers, where it often spreads vigorously if not contained.

Other Facts

Spearmint oil is used in a variety of products, including toothpaste, chewing gum, candies, and beauty products, for its refreshing scent and flavor.

Spikenard

Spikenard, also known as nard, nardin, and muskroot, is a highly aromatic herb that has been cherished for centuries for its medicinal and spiritual significance. Spikenard (Nardostachys jatamansi) is a member of the Valerian family, Valerianaceae, and is native to the high altitudes of the Himalayan mountains, particularly in Nepal, China, and India. This perennial plant is characterized by its thick, rhizome root from which the precious oil is extracted, and it bears pink, bell-shaped flowers.

Culinary Uses

While spikenard is not commonly used in mainstream culinary applications due to its strong aroma and bitter taste, it has been used traditionally in some cultures as a flavoring agent in ancient times. Its primary use in cuisine is more historical or medicinal rather than contemporary culinary applications.

Medicinal Properties

Historically, spikenard has been valued for its therapeutic properties, including its ability to calm the mind, relieve insomnia, and reduce stress and anxiety. It has been used in traditional medicine systems such as Ayurveda for its sedative and heart-tonic effects. Spikenard oil is also applied topically to improve skin conditions and promote hair growth.

Cultural Significance

Spikenard holds a prominent place in ancient texts and religious scriptures, including the Bible, where it is mentioned several times, most notably in the Song of Solomon and as the ointment with which Mary Magdalene anointed Jesus's feet. Its use in ancient Egypt for embalming and as a luxury perfume further underscores its historical and cultural value.

Production

The cultivation and harvesting of spikenard are challenging due to its specific growth requirements and the need to protect the natural habitat. The roots are harvested from mature plants, and the essential oil is extracted through steam distillation. Sustainable harvesting practices are crucial to preserve this valuable resource for future generations.

Other Facts

Spikenard essential oil is highly prized in aromatherapy for its grounding and relaxing properties. Due to its rarity and the labor-intensive extraction process, pure spikenard oil can be quite expensive.

Star anise

Star anise, known for its distinct flavor and star-shaped pods, is a cornerstone spice in various culinary traditions, particularly in Chinese and Vietnamese cuisines. Star anise (Illicium verum) belongs to the Schisandraceae family and is native to the evergreen trees of northeast Vietnam and southwest China. It is not an annual herb but a medium-sized evergreen tree, characterized by its star-shaped fruit, which contains a seed in each of its eight segments.

Culinary Uses

Star anise's flavor is warm, sweet, and licorice-like, making it a key ingredient in the Chinese five-spice powder and Vietnamese pho. It is essential in many Asian dishes for its ability to enhance meaty flavors and add depth to broths and sauces. Star anise is also used in the making of liquors such as pastis, sambuca, and anisette. In Western cuisine, it's often employed in desserts, mulled wines, and poaching liquids, imparting a sweet licorice flavor.

Medicinal Properties

Traditionally, star anise has been used in Asian medicine for its digestive, antifungal, and antibacterial properties. It is rich in antioxidants and vitamins A and C, which help boost the immune system. The spice is also a significant source of shikimic acid, which is used in the production of the antiviral drug Tamiflu.

Cultural Significance

In traditional Chinese medicine, star anise is used to treat colds and digestive issues. Its use dates back thousands of years in China, where it has been valued both for its culinary and medicinal properties. The spice plays a significant role in Chinese, Indian, and Indonesian cultural ceremonies and cooking traditions, symbolizing happiness and good fortune.

Production

Star anise is primarily produced in China and Vietnam, with China being the largest exporter of the spice. The fruit is harvested just before ripening and dried in the sun, allowing it to develop its characteristic flavor fully. The best quality star anise is recognized by its large, intact stars and a high essential oil content, which contributes to its potent flavor and aroma.

Other Facts

Star anise should not be confused with aniseed, which comes from the plant Pimpinella anisum and has a similar licorice flavor but is botanically unrelated.

Stone parsley

Stone parsley, also known as Sison amomum or burning bush, is a lesser-known herb that belongs to the Apiaceae or carrot family. It is native to Europe and parts of Asia and is characterized by its delicate, finely divided leaves and small, white or pinkish flowers that bloom in umbrella-like clusters. Unlike the more commonly known parsley (Petroselinum crispum), stone parsley is not widely used in contemporary culinary practices but has historical uses in traditional medicine and cooking.

Culinary Uses

Historically, stone parsley may have been used in traditional European cuisines for its aromatic leaves and seeds. However, its culinary use is not as prevalent or documented as other herbs like basil or common parsley. It might have been used in a similar manner to other aromatic herbs, to flavor soups, stews, and other dishes, but today it is more recognized for its ornamental or medicinal properties than for cooking.

Medicinal Properties

In traditional medicine, stone parsley has been used for its diuretic properties and to treat ailments related to the urinary tract and kidneys. Like many herbs in the Apiaceae family, it was believed to have various health benefits, although its use in modern herbal medicine is quite rare.

Cultural Significance

Stone parsley does not have the widespread cultural significance of more commonly used herbs. Its presence in historical texts and herbal compendiums mainly highlights its medicinal rather than culinary uses.

Production

Stone parsley grows in the wild across Europe and parts of Asia, typically in calcareous soils, grasslands, and along roadsides. It is not cultivated on a large scale for commercial purposes, and its use is primarily of botanical or herbal interest rather than agricultural.

Other Facts

The plant's common name, "stone parsley," may derive from its habitat preference for stony, limestone-rich soils. It should be noted that while stone parsley shares a common name with parsley, the two plants are distinct in both appearance and usage. Due to its obscurity and confusion with other plants, caution should be exercised when identifying stone parsley, since many plants in the Apiaceae family can look similar and some are toxic.

Sumac

Sumac, celebrated for its tangy, lemon-like flavor, is a staple spice in Middle Eastern and Mediterranean cuisines. Sumac comes from the berries of the Rhus coriaria shrub, which belongs to the Anacardiaceae family, native to regions of Africa, North America, and parts of Asia. It is a perennial plant, characterized by its dense clusters of red berries. The dried berries are ground into a coarse powder that is deep red or burgundy in color.

Culinary Uses

Sumac's vibrant, sour taste makes it a versatile ingredient in a variety of dishes. It is commonly used as a seasoning in salads, grilled meats, and rice dishes. Sumac is a key component in the spice mix za'atar, along with thyme, oregano, and sesame seeds. Its acidity is perfect for marinades, dressings, and to sprinkle on hummus and kebabs, adding a burst of flavor and color. Unlike lemon juice, sumac does not alter the texture of food, making it a preferred souring agent in culinary applications.

Medicinal Properties

Traditionally, sumac has been used for its health benefits, including anti-inflammatory, antioxidant, and antimicrobial properties. It is thought to help lower blood sugar levels, reduce cholesterol, and improve digestion. The high content of vitamin C in sumac also contributes to its immune-boosting effects.

Cultural Significance

Sumac has been used for centuries in Middle Eastern and Mediterranean regions, not only as a culinary spice but also for its medicinal qualities. It is often associated with hospitality and warmth in these cultures. Sumac's unique flavor profile has been celebrated in traditional cooking and continues to gain popularity worldwide as a unique and versatile spice.

Production

Sumac is harvested from the wild or cultivated in regions with a Mediterranean climate. The berries are collected just before ripening, dried, and then ground into a powder. This process ensures the preservation of sumac's tangy flavor and vibrant color.

Other Facts

Sumac is distinct from the poison sumac plant (Toxicodendron vernix), which is toxic and not related to the culinary sumac used in cooking.

Sweet woodruff

Sweet Woodruff, known for its delicate white flowers and fragrant, bright green leaves, is a cherished herb in European traditions, particularly in Germany. Sweet Woodruff (Galium odoratum) belongs to the Rubiaceae family, native to the forests of Europe and parts of Asia and North Africa. It is a perennial ground cover, celebrated not only for its aromatic qualities but also for its use in culinary, medicinal, and cultural applications.

Culinary Uses

Sweet Woodruff's flavor is slightly sweet and grassy, with hints of vanilla and fresh-cut hay, making it a unique addition to various dishes and drinks. It is famously used in Germany to flavor May wine (Maibowle), a traditional springtime beverage. The herb is also used to infuse jellies, syrups, ice creams, and teas, imparting a subtle aroma and flavor. Its leaves are sometimes used as a natural sweetener and flavoring agent in desserts and fresh salads.

Medicinal Properties

Traditionally, Sweet Woodruff has been utilized for its medicinal properties, including its ability to improve digestion, act as a diuretic, and soothe the nervous system. It has been used in herbal medicine to treat liver disorders and as a mild sedative. The coumarin content in Sweet Woodruff is responsible for its pleasant fragrance and also contributes to its use in treating headaches and insomnia.

Cultural Significance

In European folklore, Sweet Woodruff is associated with the forest and good fortune. It has been used in potpourris, natural air fresheners, and wardrobes to impart its pleasant aroma. During medieval times, it was strewn on floors to freshen up homes and churches during festivities.

Production

Sweet Woodruff thrives in shady, wooded areas, preferring moist, well-drained soil. It spreads through its root system and seed dispersal, forming dense carpets of greenery. While not commercially produced on a large scale, it is commonly cultivated in herb gardens and harvested for personal use or small-scale sale. The leaves are best harvested in spring, just before the plant flowers, when the aroma is most potent.

Tarragon

Tarragon, recognized for its distinctive, slightly sweet licorice flavor, is a perennial herb that plays a crucial role in French cuisine. Tarragon (Artemisia dracunculus) belongs to the Asteraceae family and is native to various regions across Eurasia and North America. It is characterized by its slender, elongated leaves and, in the summer, small yellow or greenish flowers. There are a few varieties, including French tarragon, which is favored for its superior flavor, and Russian tarragon, which is hardier but less flavorful.

Culinary Uses

Tarragon's unique taste is essential in many classic French dishes, such as Béarnaise sauce, and it is one of the herbs in the fines herbes blend, alongside parsley, chervil, and chives. It pairs wonderfully with chicken, fish, eggs, and is often used in salad dressings and marinades. Fresh tarragon leaves are preferred in cooking for their more intense aroma and flavor compared to dried tarragon, which can become bitter. The herb is also infused into vinegars, lending a delicate aniseed flavor.

Medicinal Properties

Traditionally, tarragon has been used for its digestive and sedative properties. It is thought to stimulate the appetite, relieve indigestion, and help with sleep disorders. Tarragon contains antioxidants and nutrients like vitamin A and C, which contribute to its health benefits, including promoting heart health and potentially lowering blood sugar levels.

Cultural Significance

Tarragon has been cultivated for centuries for both its culinary and medicinal uses. In medieval Europe, it was commonly grown in herb gardens, and its name is derived from the French word "estragon," meaning "little dragon," possibly referring to its serpentine root system or to ancient beliefs in its ability to cure snake bites.

Production

Tarragon thrives in sunny, well-drained locations and can be grown in temperate climates worldwide. French tarragon, the variety most cherished by chefs, does not produce viable seeds and is propagated through root division or cuttings. The herb is harvested by picking the leaves as needed, which can be done throughout the growing season.

Tasmanian pepper

Tasmanian pepper, known for its intense flavor and heat, is a unique spice native to the cool rainforests of Tasmania and southeastern Australia. Tasmanian pepper (Tasmannia lanceolata) belongs to the Winteraceae family and is characterized by its dark purple berries and glossy green leaves. The plant is a dioecious evergreen shrub or small tree, producing clusters of small, creamy-white flowers before the berries develop.

Culinary Uses

Tasmanian pepper's berries and leaves are both used in cooking, offering a complex flavor profile with a spicy kick, fruity notes, and a lingering warmth. The dried, ground berries are used as a spice in various dishes, including meats, cheeses, and sauces, imparting a unique peppery taste with hints of woodiness and a slightly floral aroma. The leaves can also be used fresh or dried as a herb, adding depth to slow-cooked dishes, soups, and stews. Tasmanian pepper is particularly appreciated in gourmet cooking and artisanal food products for its distinctive flavor and as a native Australian alternative to traditional pepper.

Medicinal Properties

Traditionally, Tasmanian pepper has been used by Indigenous Australians for its medicinal properties, including treating stomach aches and skin disorders. The spice contains polygodial, a compound known for its antimicrobial and anti-inflammatory effects, making it beneficial for soothing sore throats and aiding in digestive health.

Cultural Significance

Tasmanian pepper holds cultural importance in Australia, particularly among Indigenous communities, who have used it for both culinary and medicinal purposes for thousands of years. Its recent rise in popularity among chefs and food enthusiasts highlights a growing appreciation for native Australian ingredients.

Production

Tasmanian pepper is harvested from wild populations and through cultivation within Tasmania and other suitable cool, moist regions of Australia. The berries are typically harvested in late summer to autumn when they are ripe, then dried and either sold whole or ground. Sustainable harvesting practices are important to preserve wild populations and their natural habitat.

Thyme

Thyme, renowned for its earthy and slightly floral flavor, is a staple herb in many cuisines, especially in the Mediterranean, French, and Italian dishes. Thyme (Thymus vulgaris) belongs to the mint family, Lamiaceae, and is native to southern Europe from the western Mediterranean to southern Italy. It is a perennial herb, characterized by its small, aromatic green leaves, woody stems, and, in summer, tiny white or pink flowers that attract bees.

Culinary Uses

Thyme's flavor is subtle yet complex, with hints of mint, lemon, and earthiness, making it a versatile herb in cooking. It is a key ingredient in the bouquet garni and herbes de Provence in French cuisine and is used to season meats, soups, stews, and marinades. Thyme pairs well with lamb, poultry, and tomatoes, and is often used in roasting or grilling to infuse dishes with its distinctive aroma. Both fresh and dried thyme leaves are used in cooking, with the fresh leaves offering a more nuanced flavor.

Medicinal Properties

Traditionally, thyme has been used for its medicinal properties, including its ability to aid digestion, relieve coughs, and act as an antiseptic. Thymol, one of thyme's essential oils, is known for its antibacterial and antifungal properties, making it beneficial in treating infections and promoting overall health. Thyme tea is commonly used as a natural remedy for sore throats and respiratory issues.

Cultural Significance

Thyme has been used since ancient times, not only for culinary and medicinal purposes but also in cultural and religious ceremonies. It was a symbol of courage in ancient Greece, used in embalming by the Egyptians, and associated with bravery in medieval Europe. Thyme's enduring presence in gardens and kitchens underscores its significance across cultures and centuries.

Production

Thyme is cultivated worldwide in temperate climates, both in herb gardens and commercially. It thrives in well-drained soil and full sun, making it suitable for cultivation in a range of environments. Thyme is harvested for its leaves, which can be used fresh, dried, or distilled into essential oil.

Tonka beans

Tonka beans, known for their intoxicating fragrance and complex flavor profile, have emerged as a prized ingredient in high-end culinary and perfumery applications. Derived from the seeds of the Dipteryx odorata tree, a member of the pea family, Fabaceae, tonka beans are native to the rainforests of Central and South America. The beans are elongated, wrinkled, and black, with a smooth, brown interior.

Culinary Uses

Tonka beans are celebrated for their rich aroma and flavors, reminiscent of vanilla, almonds, cinnamon, and cloves, making them a versatile spice in both savory and sweet dishes. They are finely grated and used sparingly to flavor desserts such as custards, ice creams, pastries, and chocolate confections. Tonka beans also find their way into gourmet sauces and infused spirits, offering a unique depth and warmth to culinary creations.

Medicinal Properties

Historically, tonka beans have been used in traditional medicine for their anticoagulant properties. However, due to the presence of coumarin, which can be toxic in high doses, the use of tonka beans is regulated in food products in some countries.

Cultural Significance

In their native regions, tonka beans have been used not only for their flavor but also in various cultural rituals and traditional remedies. The beans' unique scent has made them a valuable commodity in the perfume industry, symbolizing exoticism and luxury.

Production

The Dipteryx odorata tree blooms with fragrant flowers, which then develop into fruit pods containing the tonka beans. After harvesting, the pods are dried, allowing the beans inside to shrink and become easily extractable. While not widely cultivated on an industrial scale, tonka beans are harvested in several countries in South America, including Venezuela and Brazil.

Other Facts

Due to the restrictions on coumarin in food, the culinary use of tonka beans remains a gourmet niche. When using tonka beans, chefs and cooks must exercise caution, employing only a tiny amount to impart flavor without exceeding recommended coumarin levels.

Turmeric

Turmeric, renowned for its vibrant golden hue and earthy flavor, is a cornerstone spice in many global cuisines, most notably in South Asian and Middle Eastern dishes. Turmeric (Curcuma longa) belongs to the ginger family, Zingiberaceae, and is native to the Indian subcontinent and Southeast Asia. It is a perennial herb, characterized by its bright yellow-orange rhizomes (rootstalks), which are ground into the powdered spice commonly used in cooking.

Culinary Uses

Turmeric's warm, bitter taste and mustard-like aroma make it a key ingredient in curries, giving them their distinctive color and flavor. It is also used in rice dishes, soups, and sauces, as well as to season meats and vegetables. In addition to its culinary uses, turmeric is a primary component of spice blends such as curry powder and is used in the preparation of mustards, pickles, and as a natural food coloring. Its subtle flavor complements a wide range of ingredients, making it a versatile spice in both savory and sweet dishes.

Medicinal Properties

Traditionally, turmeric has been used in Ayurvedic and traditional Chinese medicine for its anti-inflammatory, antioxidant, and healing properties. The compound curcumin, which gives turmeric its yellow color, is credited with much of its medicinal benefits, including potential roles in reducing inflammation, combating oxidative stress, and contributing to the prevention of chronic diseases. Turmeric is also used in natural remedies for digestive issues, wounds, and skin conditions.

Cultural Significance

Turmeric holds a significant place in many cultures, not only for its culinary and medicinal uses but also in religious and ceremonial practices. In India, it is considered auspicious and sacred, used in wedding rituals and other ceremonies. Its historical and cultural roots run deep, symbolizing purity, fertility, and the sun.

Production

India is the largest producer, consumer, and exporter of turmeric in the world. The plant thrives in tropical climates with ample rainfall and is cultivated in various parts of Asia and Africa. The rhizomes are harvested annually, boiled or steamed, and then dried and ground into powder. Fresh turmeric root is also used in cooking and natural dyes.

Vanilla

Vanilla, cherished for its sweet, aromatic flavor, is a fundamental ingredient in desserts and perfumes worldwide. Vanilla comes from the orchids of the genus Vanilla, with Vanilla planifolia being the most widely used species. Originally native to Mexico, vanilla is now grown in tropical regions around the globe, with Madagascar, Indonesia, and Tahiti being notable producers. The plant is a perennial vine that can grow quite long, producing orchid-like flowers that are pollinated by hand in cultivation.

Culinary Uses

Vanilla's warm, rich flavor and scent make it a prized ingredient in baking, cooking, and in the creation of confectionery and beverages. It is essential in dishes ranging from cakes, cookies, and ice cream to custards and puddings. Vanilla is also used to enhance the flavor of beverages such as coffee, tea, and soft drinks, as well as in savory dishes to add a depth of flavor. The spice is available in several forms, including whole pods, powder, extract, and paste, each offering different levels of intensity and complexity of flavor.

Medicinal Properties

Traditionally, vanilla has been used for its medicinal properties, including as an aphrodisiac and to aid in digestion. While not as prominently recognized for its health benefits as some other herbs and spices, vanilla contains small amounts of antioxidants and has been studied for its potential to reduce inflammation and improve mental health through its calming aroma.

Cultural Significance

Vanilla has a rich history and cultural significance, especially among the Totonac people of Mexico, who are credited with its cultivation and use before the arrival of Spanish explorers. Vanilla was once so valuable that it was used as a currency and a tribute to Aztec kings. Today, it remains a symbol of luxury and indulgence in many cultures.

Production

Vanilla cultivation is labor-intensive, requiring each flower to be hand-pollinated. After pollination, the pods take several months to mature, after which they are harvested, cured, and dried–a process that develops the vanilla beans' complex flavors. This meticulous process contributes to vanilla's status as the second most expensive spice after saffron.

Voatsiperifery

Voatsiperifery, a rare and exotic pepper, is native to the rainforests of Madagascar. Unlike common black pepper (Piper nigrum), Voatsiperifery comes from the Piper borbonense plant, a wild and climbing vine that thrives in the ecosystem's canopy. The name "Voatsiperifery" is derived from the Malagasy words for pepper (voa) and the tree it grows on (tsiperifery), highlighting its unique origin. The pepper is characterized by its small, elongated berries that grow on thin stems, harvested by hand from tall trees, which contributes to its rarity and value.

Culinary Uses

Voatsiperifery's flavor profile is complex, offering a piquant taste with woody, floral, and citrus notes, and a slightly earthy aroma. It's more aromatic and less pungent than traditional black pepper, making it a sought-after spice among chefs and gourmets. It enhances the flavor of both savory and sweet dishes, from meats and seafood to desserts and chocolates. Its unique taste also complements sauces, soups, and marinades, adding a distinctive twist to conventional recipes.

Medicinal Properties

While specific medicinal properties of Voatsiperifery are not as documented as those of common black pepper, it is believed to share some of the health benefits due to its piperine content, such as anti-inflammatory and antioxidant effects. Traditional uses in Madagascar include its application in herbal remedies for digestive issues and to improve general well-being.

Cultural Significance

Voatsiperifery is a symbol of Madagascar's rich biodiversity and traditional foraging practices. It is relatively unknown outside of Madagascar, but its recent introduction to international markets has brought attention to the island's unique flora and the importance of sustainable harvesting practices to ensure its preservation.

Production

The production of Voatsiperifery is limited due to its wild growth and the challenging harvesting conditions, as the berries must be picked by hand from the tops of tall trees. This labor-intensive process, along with its limited geographic availability, makes Voatsiperifery a rare and premium spice. Efforts to cultivate it outside of its natural habitat have not been widely successful, preserving its status as a wild-harvested product.

Wasabi

Wasabi, known for its sharp, pungent flavor, is a staple condiment in Japanese cuisine, closely associated with sushi and sashimi. Wasabi (Wasabia japonica) belongs to the Brassicaceae family, which also includes mustard, horseradish, and cabbage. Native to Japan, it is a perennial plant that grows naturally along stream beds in mountain river valleys. The part most commonly used is the rhizome, which is grated into a fine paste.

Culinary Uses

Wasabi's intense heat and unique flavor make it an essential accompaniment to sushi and sashimi, helping to enhance the taste of the fish and cleanse the palate. Unlike the heat from chili peppers, which lingers, wasabi's heat is more volatile and dissipates quickly. Wasabi is also used in other dishes such as soba noodles, salads, and as a flavoring in snacks like peas and nuts. Its distinct taste comes from the compounds called isothiocyanates, which are released when the rhizome is grated.

Medicinal Properties

Traditionally, wasabi has been credited with various health benefits, including anti-microbial properties that can help inhibit the growth of bacteria and fungi. It is also thought to have anti-inflammatory effects and may aid in detoxification. The isothiocyanates in wasabi have been studied for their potential anti-cancer properties, although more research is needed to fully understand these effects.

Cultural Significance

Wasabi is deeply ingrained in Japanese culture and cuisine, symbolizing tradition, natural beauty, and the country's culinary heritage. The traditional method of grating wasabi using a sharkskin grater (oroshigane) is considered an art form, reflecting the importance of presentation and preparation in Japanese cooking.

Production

True wasabi is notoriously difficult to cultivate, requiring a specific set of conditions to grow: clean, running water, shade, and a cool, humid environment. Most wasabi served outside Japan is actually a mixture of horseradish, mustard, and green food coloring, as genuine wasabi is expensive and loses its potency quickly after grating. Japan remains the largest producer of wasabi, with some cultivation also occurring in Taiwan, Korea, New Zealand, and parts of the United States and Canada.

Water-pepper

Water-pepper, also known as Polygonum hydropiper, is a lesser-known but intriguing herb belonging to the Polygonaceae family. Native to temperate regions of the Northern Hemisphere, including North America, Europe, and Asia, water-pepper is an annual herb characterized by its slender stems, lance-shaped leaves, and small, greenish-white or pink flowers. The plant thrives in wet conditions, often found growing along stream banks and in marshy areas.

Culinary Uses

Water-pepper's flavor is distinctly sharp and spicy, with a heat that can rival that of some chili peppers. Its leaves and seeds are used in small quantities to add a peppery kick to salads, soups, and sauces. In Japan, the leaves are traditionally used as a spice in certain dishes, such as sashimi, where they complement the dish's flavors with their unique pungency. The intensity of water-pepper makes it a spice that should be used sparingly, allowing its heat to enhance rather than overpower the overall taste of a dish.

Medicinal Properties

Traditionally, water-pepper has been valued for its medicinal properties, including its use as an anti-inflammatory, diuretic, and stimulant. It has been used in herbal medicine to treat digestive issues, menstrual pain, and various other ailments. The plant contains compounds such as polygodial, which contribute to its spicy taste and medicinal effects.

Cultural Significance

While not as widely recognized as other herbs and spices, water-pepper holds a place in the traditional culinary and medicinal practices of the regions where it is native. Its use in local cuisines and healing traditions underscores the diversity of plants valued for their flavor and therapeutic properties.

Production

Water-pepper is not widely cultivated on a commercial scale but is often harvested from the wild or grown in small herb gardens. The plant's preference for wet, marshy conditions makes it a unique addition to water gardens or naturalized areas where its growth conditions can be met. Harvesting typically involves collecting the leaves and seeds when the plant is in bloom, ensuring the highest potency of its spicy constituents.

Wattleseed

Wattleseed, an indigenous Australian ingredient, comes from various species of the Acacia tree, notable for its culinary and nutritional value. This versatile spice has been used by Aboriginal Australians for thousands of years, both as a source of food and for medicinal purposes. The seeds are harvested from the pods of the Acacia, then traditionally ground into a flour-like consistency.

Culinary Uses

Wattleseed's flavor is complex and has been described as nutty, with hints of coffee, chocolate, and hazelnut, making it a unique addition to a wide array of dishes. It is used in baking bread, cakes, and biscuits, and as a seasoning in savory dishes. Wattleseed is also employed in the preparation of sauces, marinades, and dressings, imparting a deep, aromatic flavor. Its versatility extends to desserts and beverages, where it adds richness to ice creams, custards, and even coffee and smoothies.

Medicinal Properties

Traditionally, wattleseed has been valued for its high protein and carbohydrate content, serving as a nutritious staple in the diets of indigenous Australians. While specific medicinal benefits vary among the different Acacia species, wattleseed generally contains antioxidants, minerals, and fibers, supporting digestive health and overall well-being.

Cultural Significance

Wattleseed holds significant cultural importance for Aboriginal Australians, representing a connection to the land and traditional practices of foraging and food preparation. It is a symbol of the rich biodiversity of Australia and the knowledge and traditions of its indigenous peoples.

Production

The production of wattleseed involves the collection of seed pods from the Acacia trees, which are then dried and the seeds extracted. Modern methods have adapted to include mechanical processing for larger scale production, but many communities still practice traditional harvesting methods. Australia remains the primary source of wattleseed, with increased interest in native ingredients contributing to its availability on the global market.

Wild thyme

Wild thyme, known for its intense and aromatic flavor, is a perennial herb that thrives in various regions, especially in the Mediterranean. Wild thyme (Thymus serpyllum), also known as creeping thyme, belongs to the mint family, Lamiaceae, and is characterized by its small, fragrant leaves and purple or pink flowers. It grows low to the ground, forming mats that can cover large areas in wild landscapes.

Culinary Uses

Wild thyme's flavor is robust, with a more pronounced earthiness compared to common thyme (Thymus vulgaris). It is used in a variety of culinary applications, including seasoning meats, soups, and stews. Wild thyme is particularly beloved in Mediterranean cuisine, where it contributes to the flavor profiles of traditional dishes. It pairs well with lamb, poultry, and vegetables, and can also be used in marinades and herbal blends. The herb is often used dried, but fresh wild thyme offers a milder taste that can enhance salads and garnishes.

Medicinal Properties

Traditionally, wild thyme has been valued for its medicinal properties, including antiseptic, antifungal, and anti-inflammatory effects. It has been used to treat respiratory issues, sore throats, and digestive problems. The herb contains thymol, an essential oil with powerful antimicrobial properties, making it beneficial for overall health and wellness.

Cultural Significance

In various cultures, wild thyme is associated with courage and bravery. It has a rich history in folk medicine and has been used in spiritual practices for purification and protection. In Mediterranean regions, wild thyme is a symbol of the rugged landscapes and the resilience of the plants that thrive there.

Production

Wild thyme is commonly found growing in natural, uncultivated areas, including rocky hillsides and grasslands. While it is not typically farmed on a large scale, wild thyme can be cultivated in gardens for personal use. It prefers full sun and well-drained soil and is drought-tolerant once established. The herb is harvested for its leaves and flowering tops, which are most flavorful just before the plant blooms.

Wintergreen

Wintergreen, known for its refreshing, minty flavor, is a perennial herb native to North America's wooded and mountainous regions. Wintergreen (Gaultheria procumbens) belongs to the Ericaceae family and is characterized by its glossy, dark green leaves, white bell-shaped flowers, and bright red berries. The plant's common name comes from its ability to maintain its vibrant green color throughout the winter.

Culinary Uses

Wintergreen's leaves and berries are used in small quantities to flavor candies, chewing gum, toothpaste, and some medicinal teas. The leaves are steeped to make wintergreen tea, a traditional herbal beverage. Its oil, methyl salicylate, is extracted from the leaves and used as a flavoring agent in various food products, offering a cooling, sweet taste reminiscent of peppermint but with a distinctively woodsy undertone.

Medicinal Properties

Historically, wintergreen has been used for its analgesic and anti-inflammatory properties. Methyl salicylate, the active compound in wintergreen, is similar to aspirin and has been used topically as a pain reliever for muscular and joint discomfort. Wintergreen oil is also used in aromatherapy for its soothing effects and to relieve respiratory conditions.

Cultural Significance

Wintergreen has played a role in the traditional medicine of Indigenous peoples of North America, who used it for various ailments, including headaches, fever, and sore throats. It continues to be valued for its medicinal benefits and is a popular natural remedy in herbal medicine.

Production

Wintergreen is not widely cultivated on a commercial scale but is harvested from the wild. The extraction of wintergreen oil is primarily from the leaves, which are fermented to increase the methyl salicylate content before distillation. Sustainable harvesting practices are important to ensure the longevity of wild wintergreen populations.

Other Facts

Wintergreen oil must be used with caution, as it can be toxic if ingested in large quantities or used improperly on the skin. It is also used in liniments and ointments for its warming effect and pain-relieving properties.

Wood avens

Wood avens, also known as Geum urbanum or herb bennet, is a perennial herb native to Europe and parts of Asia and North Africa. Belonging to the Rosaceae family, wood avens is characterized by its hairy stems, pinnate leaves, and small yellow flowers that bloom from spring to early summer. The plant is commonly found in woodlands, hedgerows, and shady gardens, thriving in moist, well-drained soil.

Culinary Uses

The roots of wood avens, which have a clove-like aroma, are used in traditional cooking to flavor soups, stews, and beers. While not widely used in modern cuisine, the roots can be dried and powdered as a spice or used fresh. The young leaves can also be added to salads or used as a herb in cooking for their slight bitterness, which adds depth to dishes.

Medicinal Properties

Traditionally, wood avens has been valued for its medicinal properties, including its use as an antiseptic, astringent, and digestive aid. The root, in particular, is known to help treat gastrointestinal issues, sore throats, and was used as a remedy for diarrhea and fevers. Its antiseptic properties make it useful in herbal medicine for treating minor wounds and infections.

Cultural Significance

In medieval Europe, wood avens was believed to offer protection against evil spirits and was often planted around homes and churches for this purpose. It was also carried by travelers as a talisman for safe journeys. The plant holds a place in folklore as a symbol of luck and prosperity.

Production

Wood avens is not typically cultivated on a large scale for commercial use but can be grown in herb gardens for personal use. The plant propagates by seed and can spread through its rhizome roots, forming dense clumps over time. Harvesting usually involves collecting the roots in autumn or early spring when the plant's aromatic compounds are most concentrated.

Other Facts

In addition to its culinary and medicinal uses, wood avens is appreciated for its ornamental value in gardens, attracting bees and butterflies with its flowers. The plant's roots were historically used as a substitute for cloves, hence one of its other common names, "clove root."

Woodruff

Woodruff, known for its sweet, hay-like fragrance, is a perennial herb cherished in various European traditions. Woodruff (Galium odoratum) belongs to the Rubiaceae family and is native to Europe, North Africa, and Western Asia. It thrives in woodland environments, characterized by its whorled leaves and small, white, star-shaped flowers.

Culinary Uses

Woodruff's unique flavor is a key component in traditional European cuisine, notably in Germany, where it flavors the springtime beverage Maibowle (May wine). Its aromatic qualities are infused into syrups, jellies, ice creams, and other desserts. Dried woodruff leaves are used to impart a vanilla-like flavor to cakes, custards, and teas. The herb's subtle sweetness complements dairy products and can be used as a garnish for fresh fruit and salads.

Medicinal Properties

Traditionally, woodruff has been valued for its potential medicinal benefits, including its use as a mild sedative, diuretic, and liver tonic. It contains coumarin, which contributes to its pleasant aroma and was historically used to freshen homes and linens. In herbal medicine, woodruff is believed to aid digestion and promote heart health, although its use should be moderated due to coumarin's potential health effects at high concentrations.

Cultural Significance

Woodruff holds a special place in folklore and herbalism, associated with purity, protection, and healing. It was used in medieval times as a strewing herb to deodorize and sanitize indoor spaces. The celebration of woodruff in May wine links it to spring festivals and traditions celebrating renewal and vitality.

Production

Woodruff is harvested in the wild and cultivated in herb gardens for its leaves and flowers. The best time to harvest woodruff is just before or during its flowering stage when the concentration of aromatic compounds is highest. Drying the herb enhances its fragrance and flavor, making it a staple in the dried herb pantry.

Wormwood

Wormwood, known for its bitter flavor and aromatic qualities, is a perennial herb that plays a significant role in herbal medicine and the production of spirits. Wormwood (Artemisia absinthium) belongs to the Asteraceae family and is native to temperate regions of Europe, Asia, and North Africa. It is characterized by its silvery-green leaves, yellow-green flowers, and a distinctive bitter taste.

Culinary Uses

The culinary uses of wormwood are primarily linked to its role in the production of absinthe, a potent spirit historically associated with bohemian culture and creativity. Wormwood contributes the characteristic bitter flavor to absinthe and other traditional liqueurs and bitters. While not commonly used in cooking due to its intense bitterness, small amounts of wormwood may be used to flavor certain dishes, imparting a unique herbal note.

Medicinal Properties

Traditionally, it has been used in herbal medicine to stimulate appetite, aid digestion, and treat a variety of ailments, including liver and gallbladder conditions. The active compound thujone in wormwood is thought to be responsible for its medicinal effects, though it can be toxic in high doses.

Cultural Significance

Wormwood was used in ancient times to ward off evil spirits and disease, and it has been a common ingredient in traditional medicine across many cultures. The controversy and mystique surrounding absinthe, partly due to wormwood's psychoactive properties, have further cemented its place in cultural history.

Production

Wormwood is cultivated in herb gardens and commercially for its use in absinthe and other herbal products. It thrives in poor, dry soil and full sun, making it relatively easy to grow in suitable climates. The plant is harvested for its leaves and flowering tops, which are dried for use in distillation, tinctures, and teas.

Other Facts

Due to the potential toxicity of thujone, wormwood and absinthe were banned in many countries in the early 20th century, though recent regulations have allowed their controlled use.

Yerba Buena

Yerba Buena, known for its refreshing and aromatic qualities, is a versatile herb widely used in traditional medicine and culinary applications across various cultures. Yerba Buena refers to several species within the mint family, Lamiaceae, but most commonly to Clinopodium douglasii (also known as Mentha arvensis in some regions). It is native to North and South America but has been naturalized in many parts of the world, including the Philippines, where it is popular in traditional remedies.

Culinary Uses

Yerba Buena's flavor is cool and minty, with a slightly sweet undertone, making it a popular addition to beverages, cocktails, and culinary dishes. It is used to flavor mojitos, teas, and other refreshing drinks. In cooking, it can be added to sauces, salads, and desserts for a burst of minty freshness. The herb pairs well with fruits, chocolates, and savory dishes, offering a versatile range of uses in the kitchen.

Medicinal Properties

Traditionally, Yerba Buena has been valued for its medicinal properties, including its ability to relieve pain, soothe digestive issues, and reduce fever. It is often used as a natural remedy for headaches, colds, and stomach aches. The herb's essential oils have anti-inflammatory and analgesic properties, making it a common ingredient in natural health products.

Cultural Significance

Yerba Buena holds a significant place in traditional medicine systems, particularly in Latin American and Filipino cultures. It is often grown in home gardens and used in household remedies, reflecting its importance in daily health and wellness practices. The herb's name, which translates to "good herb" in Spanish, underscores its valued status among various communities.

Production

Yerba Buena is cultivated in herb gardens and can also be found growing wild in suitable climates. It thrives in moist, shaded areas and can be easily propagated from cuttings, making it accessible for home cultivation. The leaves are harvested for their aromatic oils, which are most potent when the plant is in bloom.

Other Facts

Yerba Buena is also used in aromatherapy and as a natural insect repellent due to its strong minty aroma.

Yarrow

Yarrow, known for its healing properties and delicate, feathery foliage, is a perennial herb that has been valued in herbal medicine for centuries. Yarrow (Achillea millefolium) belongs to the Asteraceae family and is native to temperate regions of the Northern Hemisphere, including Europe, Asia, and North America. It is characterized by its white to pinkish flowers arranged in compact clusters and its aromatic, finely divided leaves.

Culinary Uses

While not as commonly used in cooking as other herbs, yarrow can be used in culinary applications for its bitter and slightly aromatic flavor. It can be added to salads, soups, and teas, providing a subtle herbaceous note. Its young leaves are the most suitable for culinary use, as older leaves can become too bitter. Yarrow is also occasionally used in the production of bitters and other herbal liqueurs.

Medicinal Properties

Yarrow is renowned for its wide range of medicinal properties. It has been used traditionally to stop bleeding, heal wounds, and reduce inflammation. Yarrow contains several beneficial compounds, including flavonoids and salicylic acid, which contribute to its anti-inflammatory, analgesic, and antiseptic qualities. It is also used to aid digestion, reduce fever, and relieve cold and flu symptoms.

Cultural Significance

The herb's name, Achillea, derives from the mythical Greek hero Achilles, who supposedly used yarrow to treat his soldiers' wounds, highlighting its long history of use in wound healing. Yarrow holds a place in folklore and traditional medicine across many cultures, symbolizing healing, protection, and love.

Production

Yarrow is found growing wild in meadows, fields, and along roadsides, but it can also be cultivated in gardens for its ornamental and medicinal qualities. It prefers well-drained soil and full sun and is drought-tolerant once established. Yarrow is harvested for its flowers and leaves, which can be used fresh or dried for later use.

Za'atar

Za'atar, the herb, refers to a type of wild thyme native to the Middle East, scientifically known as Origanum syriacum. It belongs to the mint family, Lamiaceae, and is closely related to thyme, oregano, and marjoram. This perennial herb is characterized by its small, gray-green leaves and delicate purple flowers, known for their distinctive and pungent aroma.

Culinary Uses

Za'atar herb is celebrated for its unique flavor, which is both earthy and tangy, with a hint of nuttiness. It is a key ingredient in the traditional Middle Eastern za'atar spice blend, where it is mixed with sumac, sesame seeds, and salt. The herb alone can be used fresh or dried to season meats, vegetables, and breads. It is particularly popular in Levantine cuisine, where it's sprinkled over labneh (yogurt cheese), mixed into doughs, or used as a rub for grilled meats.

Medicinal Properties

Traditionally, za'atar has been used for its medicinal properties, including its ability to improve digestion, boost cognitive function, and reduce inflammation. The herb is rich in antioxidants, vitamins, and minerals, contributing to its health benefits. It has also been used as an antiseptic and for respiratory health in folk medicine.

Cultural Significance

Za'atar holds a special place in Middle Eastern culture, not just as a culinary staple but also for its symbolic value. It is associated with hospitality and comfort, often served with bread and olive oil to guests. The herb and its namesake spice blend are integral to daily life in many Middle Eastern countries, embodying the region's rich flavors and culinary traditions.

Production

Za'atar herb is harvested from the wild in the Levant and parts of North Africa, though it is also cultivated in gardens and farms to meet culinary demand. The plant thrives in sunny, dry conditions and well-drained soil, making it well-suited to the Mediterranean climate. Harvesting typically involves collecting the leaves and flowering tops, which are then dried for later use.

Zedoary

Zedoary, a lesser-known yet valuable herb, is celebrated for its culinary and medicinal qualities. Zedoary (Curcuma zedoaria) belongs to the ginger family, Zingiberaceae, and is native to India and Indonesia. It is a perennial herb characterized by its large, white or yellow flowers and long, bright green leaves. The rhizome, or underground stem, is the most utilized part of the plant, similar in appearance to ginger but with a white interior and a strong, woody aroma.

Culinary Uses

Zedoary's flavor is warm and bitter, with hints of ginger and mango. It is primarily used in traditional Southeast Asian and Indian cuisines, where it adds a unique flavor to curries, rice dishes, and pickles. The rhizome can be used fresh, dried, or powdered. In some regions, it is also used as a substitute for arrowroot as a thickening agent. Its distinctive taste complements both meat and vegetarian dishes, enhancing flavors with its aromatic presence.

Medicinal Properties

Traditionally, zedoary has been valued for its medicinal properties, including its ability to improve digestion, relieve flatulence, and stimulate appetite. It is believed to have anti-inflammatory and antimicrobial effects, making it useful in treating infections and various health conditions. Zedoary is also used in Ayurvedic and traditional Chinese medicine to support liver health and as an antioxidant.

Cultural Significance

In its native regions, zedoary has been used for centuries not only as a culinary spice but also in rituals and traditional medicine. It is considered a symbol of health and longevity, reflecting its deep-rooted cultural and medicinal importance.

Production

Zedoary is cultivated in tropical climates, with India and Southeast Asia being the primary producers. The rhizomes are harvested, cleaned, and then either dried or ground into powder for culinary and medicinal use. Cultivation and harvesting are generally done using traditional methods that preserve the natural qualities of the herb.

Other Facts

In addition to its use in food and medicine, zedoary is sometimes included in perfumes and cosmetics for its fragrance and potential skin benefits.

Made in the USA
Las Vegas, NV
03 August 2024